THE ESSENTIAL CONCEPT of LAW

| TEACHING TEXTS IN LAW AND POLITICS |

David A. Schultz
General Editor

Vol. 33

PETER LANG
New York • Washington, D.C./Baltimore • Bern
Frankfurt am Main • Berlin • Brussels • Vienna • Oxford

JAMES T. McHUGH

THE ESSENTIAL CONCEPT of LAW

PETER LANG
New York • Washington, D.C./Baltimore • Bern
Frankfurt am Main • Berlin • Brussels • Vienna • Oxford

Library of Congress Cataloging-in-Publication Data
McHugh, James T.
The essential concept of law / James T. McHugh.
p. cm. — (Teaching texts in law and politics; v. 33)
Includes bibliographical references and index.
1. Law. 2. Comparative law. I. Title. II. Series.
K559 .M38   340—dc21   2002070492
ISBN 0-8204-6180-6
ISSN 1083-3447

Die Deutsche Bibliothek-CIP-Einheitsaufnahme
McHugh, James T.:
The essential concept of law / James T. McHugh.
−New York; Washington, D.C./Baltimore; Bern;
Frankfurt am Main; Berlin; Brussels; Vienna; Oxford: Lang.
(Teaching texts in law and politics; Vol. 33)
ISBN 0-8204-6180-6

Cover design by Dutton & Sherman Design

© 2002 Peter Lang Publishing, Inc., New York

All rights reserved.
Reprint or reproduction, even partially, in all forms such as microfilm,
xerography, microfiche, microcard, and offset strictly prohibited.

Table of Contents

Acknowledgments vii

1 The Universal Idea of Law 1
2 Western Legal Heritage 9
3 Eastern Legal Heritage 23
4 Ideology and Law 35
5 Common Law Systems 53
6 Civil Law Systems 69
7 Western Religion and Its Law 85
8 Tribal Law 97
9 Unitary, Federal, and Confederal Systems 105
10 Crime, Injury, Punishment, and the State 113
11 Property and Contract 125
12 Rights and Liberties 133
13 The Moral Idea of Law 147

Bibliography 153
Index 159

Acknowledgments

I would like to thank Dr. David Schultz, the series editor, for his advice and encouragement. I also would like to thank Bernadette Alfaro, Phyllis Korper, and everyone at Peter Lang who provided me with assistance and encouragement in preparing this manuscript for publication. I further want to thank Michelle Parker and Kimberly Kunio of Roosevelt University for their valuable technical assistance. I remain, as always, grateful for the support and encouragement of my family toward this process and all my endeavors.

CHAPTER 1

The Universal Idea of Law

Law as an Idea

Popular attitudes toward law often present it as the exclusive domain of professional practitioners. However, all legal activity derives its authority from a body of *public* law, and that term affirms the fact that law is, indeed, an idea that is derived from, and directed toward, the political community. Law belongs, therefore, to all people, especially within a society in which they constitute, collectively, the ultimate expression of sovereign authority through democratic institutions. A people who abdicate an understanding of, and responsibility for, the law to a parochial body of professional practitioners deny themselves the power that is the true source and purpose of law. Furthermore, they help to obscure the valid underlying nature of law by confusing its foundational ideals with its technical expression and practice. Law, as an idea, belongs to everyone, for it reflects their collective ideals.

Law always has been subject to misconceptions, particularly concerning its fundamental nature and purpose. Many modern observers often tend to associate law with mere rules. Consequently, those observers tend to presume that these rules may be related to certain abstract principles and methods of organization, but not to a broader, subjective, and philosophically driven theme or ideal that unifies the law. This presumption fails to acknowledge, seriously, the more genuine conception of law as an idea, itself, that can be expanded into large, yet interrelated, variations upon broader themes and premises. In fact, an appreciation of those themes and premises makes it possible to discern law in ways that are predictable, consistent, and tied to some of the most profound ideas, values, and traits that define the human experience. Law *is* an idea; specific laws are, merely, an extrapolation of this idea of law and a manifestation of a higher purpose which the law, *as* an ultimate idea, seeks to achieve.

In a very real sense, law is *not* created by legal practitioners; it is created by a political people, within a political environment, for a purpose that is, definitively, political. That concept may seem simple to accept, yet many, perhaps most, people seem to regard law as a technical field that is relevant while being, simultaneously, external to their experience. In that way, it can be related to a typical response to industrial and post-industrial technology, for people have become dependent upon it, but they also believe that it is grounded upon abstractions that are so complex and alien to their normal existence that a critical appraisal of it is not relevant to their daily existence. That fallacy is extremely damaging to the law and the people it should serve, for it removes them from something that is, in fact, intimately connected to themselves and those things that most profoundly define them as social beings and, even, as humans. W. H. Auden expressed this sentiment within his 1939 poem, "Law Like Love."[1] Auden used his poem to describe various ways in which law has been experienced and applied. Although his purpose was to draw a broader parallel between the law and a more profound emotional realm, he offers, nonetheless, insights into different legal traditions and ideas. The concepts introduced within the first part of his poem address themes that will be considered throughout this book.

Law first is associated by Auden with the natural world that governs the seasons in a cyclical, and largely predictable, pattern. It also is associated with the authority that comes with experience and tradition, especially as handed down from previous generations. It also is linked to a decidedly moral foundation, based upon fundamental teachings of rights and wrong. That relationship between law and morals would be renounced by the Western legal tradition as part of the secularization of the legal realm and the development of the axiom of the separation of church and state.

Yet the political purposes of the law also are acknowledged. Law is represented as a tool of power, wielded by political elites who also shape its meaning. It is treated as something practical. It also is portrayed as coercive. Furthermore, it is perceived as being devoid of emotion and, indeed, any normative consideration of higher beliefs and values. Law is presented as rules that require no justification beyond their existence and the fact that they establish order and control that are essential to any political system—essentially, law as power.

Still, there is a recognition that law may possess a more ethereal quality that transcends its mundane purposes. Law is an idea that reflects the human condition in a very pivotal way. Therefore, it is grounded upon concepts as profound as the tenets of philosophy. It does not belong solely to the practitioner but, also, to the scholar and commentator who muse upon its larger meaning. Indeed, it belongs, consequently, to everyone, for it emanates from the most fundamental features of the human condition. In that sense, it can be linked back to that moral perspective

---

1   W. H. Auden, "Law Like Love," *Collected Poems*, Edward Mendelson, ed. (New York: Random House, 1976), p. 208.

associated with the teachings of religion and even be treated as an emanation of a divine purpose and plan.

Finally, law is presented by Auden as ultimately subjective. It is a realm of enormous contention. It can be understood, simultaneously, as a collective expression and as a source of individual protection. It does not possess the precision or certainty of the natural or physical sciences, so it is not surprising that legal practitioners may be popularly contrasted sharply with practitioners of the physical and natural sciences, including medicine. Again, though, law is one of the most human of endeavors, so making a link between it and a concept as fundamental as love (as Auden does through his poem) seems, upon reflection, quite reasonable.

This poem reveals some of the varied and complex aspects, and perceptions, of law. It can be perceived as all-encompassing, venerable, instructive, authoritative, and, even, sacred. Law also can be perceived as punitive, rule-based, controlling, and an instrument of an all-embracing power of government. Law also can be associated with a collective identity, or it can be defined from an individual perspective. It can be comforting or coercive—all of these alternative, competing claims depending upon the particular approach that is employed to define it. These varying and romantic images convey both confusion and profound insights into an enigmatic facet of the human experience that is, consummately, law.

Law as "Objectivity" and "Neutrality"

This complex, enduring, and, indeed, poetical nature of law provides a far more meaningful perspicacity than its more parochial, professional, technocratic articulation. The most enduring fallacy concerning the law, especially from that latter and, sadly, too prominent perspective, is the belief that it is, somehow, "objective." The image of the famous fictional character, Professor Kingsfield, from the film *The Paper Chase* (based upon a real, eminent, Harvard Law School professor) has become a popular portrait that often is associated with this legalistic stereotype. The menacing stress that this professor places upon his students to employ the Socratic method of logic in order to arrive at "rational" legal conclusions reinforces a popular image of law that supposedly is devoid of normative beliefs and values and is practiced and interpreted in a calculating and unemotional fashion.

According to this popular image, law is regarded as a "science" in an antiseptic way. It should be, according to this perspective, as far removed from nonempirical musings as a properly pursued analysis of physics. Finally, according to this image, law is the exclusive realm of the rigorously trained expert practitioner, whose memorization of its complex, secret language, codes, formulas, and incantations keeps it properly segregated from the unschooled masses, presumptuous elite non-practitioners, and anyone who might heretically dare to believe that law truly belongs to society. This image might make it seem that law is best left to the temperament and style of the rigidly unemotional, completely "logical," extraterrestrial race of the Vulcans, as created by the cult science-fiction television and film series *Star Trek*.

This charge against the popular image of law may seem harsh, yet it is a response to an attitude that has plagued modern societies and, quite possibly, prevented even very well-educated people from experiencing law as it truly exists. One possible basis for the problem may stem from a semantic mistake. The term "objectivity," when applied to the law, is inaccurate and misapplied; a more meaningful and accurate term, in this respect, could be legal "neutrality." It is far more possible to establish legal norms that are designed to provide for fairness than it is to separate laws from the normative values that motivated their creation. That relationship lies, in fact, at the very foundation of law, which is, essentially, a human expression of human experiences.

The notion that law is neutral can arise from those same values, especially within a society that reveres equality, competition, merit, and a search for truth. But the idea that law is objective would presuppose an absence of that very same value system and be, therefore, illogical. Law is *not* the product of a random computer model, but a way for humans and their communities to define themselves, their most fundamental convictions, and their relationships to each other. Therefore, in order to understand law, it is necessary to understand that necessarily subjective foundation.

Law and Morality: "The Search for the Grail"

Another modern preoccupation with law focuses upon its moral purposes. An "objective," or, even, a neutral, image of law tends to discount and, often, deride, such a fixation. But an association between law and morals has existed, perhaps, as long as the very idea of law. The fact that laws inevitably reflect the beliefs and values of the sovereign authority that creates and enforces them arguably makes that association unavoidable. Constitutions play the ultimate role in that process, providing a philosophical foundation for an entire political community and its political and legal systems and, in the process, defining the underlying moral purpose that guides all other public goals and aspirations. Constitutional law, in particular, and public law, in general, can provide, therefore, the paramount expression of moral expression that defines each polity.

However, the precise identification of that moral foundation generally remains elusive and subject to debate. The quest for that constitutional core can assume the symbolic proportions, and frustrations, of the medieval search for the Holy Grail, as illustrated within the legends of King Arthur and his court of Camelot. But, like that fable, the true benefit of the search for a "moral absolute" within the law (especially as expressed at the constitutional level) arrives not with the actual discovery of the Grail (which proves, ultimately, all but impossible) but with the profound insights, self-awareness, and greater clarity that occur during the process of the search. Sincere students of public law, especially as a field of political science, achieve that same benefit through a search for the core meaning and purpose of public law. Critical thinking that is greatly enhanced by such a sincere process transcends any definitive answer that might be gained, and it makes possible the connections that are revealed between constitutions, legal norms and practices, political systems, political theories, and the states, communities, and people who are, ultimately, affected by them in a definitional way.

Constitutional Law

Constitutions are the apex of a political and legal tradition. All other legal expressions of the polity emanate from a constitution. Therefore, any law that fails to conform to the standards of a constitution cannot function *as* a law. Constitutions also serve as the ultimate expression of the entire political system and, in fact, define it. They establish the fundamental principles that the guide the political system in an equally fundamental way. They also impose limits and constraints upon that same political system, so constitutions can inhibit people, but they also can liberate them. The ultimate role of a constitution thus depends upon the sovereign source of the fundamental values upon which it is based and, indeed, the precise identity of that sovereign authority. That definition also is vital for international law, as traditionally supposed.

This definition of sovereignty is, arguably, the most important concept of law and politics, and constitutions are vital to that definition. Sovereignty refers to a basis of power, exercised over the community, with no power exercised over it. Sovereignty provides states with that quality that autonomy offers to individual people. A political community cannot qualify as a "state" under international law without that sovereign identity. It is, in that sense, too, the "ultimate" law.

Sovereign status ultimately can be demonstrated only through the production and enforcement of a legitimate constitutional tradition. These constitutions produce government institutions, laws, and social conditions that constitute the modern polity. Indeed, constitutions rose simultaneously with the concept of the modern state, although constitutions existed prior to the modern period of history. But in the conventional sense, constitutional law is associated with the rise of the nation-state, modern ideologies, and, in many instances, the democratic ideal of a sovereign authority emanating from a popular source. This last development has made the study of constitutions particularly important, while also adding to their complexity, particularly in terms of identifying those fundamental values that define them.

The legal system that is derived from a constitutional tradition can be conceived as a source, and tool, of sovereign control over a political community. An international law perspective would use that conception to reduce the legal persons of those sovereign communities to mere "objects" of the law, while the sovereign state, as defined by its constitutional tradition, is recognized as a proper "subject" of the international legal community. However, a constitutional system also can be regarded as a legal source that guards against the potential abuse of that same sovereign authority against its "objects." A constitutional tradition also is a philosophical declaration of a higher ideal that unites that community; it is not merely a superior body of law, but a political statement of such fundamental importance that it cannot be divorced from its wider social, economic, political, and, even, moral foundation. Constitutional traditions are inextricably linked to the history and culture within which they have evolved.

Purpose and Plan of the Text

This book explores ideas that form the basis for all legal understanding, while the second part applies those ideas to actual constitutions of a variety of countries. It engages in a study in contrasts, beginning with very broad categorizations and narrowing toward more parochial, yet fundamental, legal concepts. It addresses law in its multitudinous facets, in order to provide a comprehensive appreciation of it. Therefore, this text often is as much about political systems, ideals, cultures, and motives as it is about a parochial, formal-legal appraisal of public law. But, then, these forces are, consummately, the genuine purpose of law, itself.

This book begins with a division of the legal world, in its broadest sense, into Western and Eastern traditions. It then examines the fundamental relationship between modern law and ideology. The book then shifts from this substantive analysis to a more structural appraisal of law as an institution, starting with the two most dominant legal structures in the world, the common law and the civil law systems. This evaluation is succeeded by an assessment of the contributions of Western religion to the idea of law, followed by an exploration of the concept of tribal law as an alternative to conventional understandings.

The book returns to a structural analysis with an explanation of unitary, federal, and confederal alternatives to sovereign legal and political expression. Themes of crime, injury, punishment, and the overall concept of the state are introduced, followed by an overview of the fundamental legal concepts of property and contract. Finally, the theme of rights and liberties, which has assumed such a conspicuous position within modern legal discourse, is evaluated. This approach encourages a conceptualization of law that appreciates the broad, underlying foundations of the law and provides true, substantive meaning to more specific legal categories that are, also, fundamental to this overall understanding.

References

Nicholas Abercrombie, Stephen Hill, and Brian S. Turner, *The Dominant Ideology Thesis*. London, George Allen and Unwin, 1985.
Aristotle, *The Politics*, Ernest Barker, trans. and ed. Oxford, Clarendon, 1952.
René David and John E. C. Brierley, *Major Legal Systems in the World Today*. New York, The Free Press, 1978.
Lon Fuller, *The Morality of Law*. New Haven, CT, Yale University Press, 1964.
Denis Lloyd [Lord Lloyd of Hampstead], *The Idea of Law*. London, Penguin, 1987.
Konrad Zweigert and Hein Kötz, *An Introduction to Comparative Law*, Toney Weir, trans. Amsterdam, North Holland, 1977

CHAPTER 2

Western Legal Heritage

East and West

The world can be divided, from a fundamental, humanly conceptual perspective, roughly into categories of "East" and "West." Law, in its broadest sense, can be divided into similarly broad categories. This conceptual distinction needs to be appreciated before other substantive legal definitions can be broached.

Scholars of cultural anthropology, comparative religion, social psychology, and other areas have identified certain broad features that distinguish Eastern and Western patterns of thought and perception, often revealed in the symbols that various cultures within this broad, and artificial, division embrace. Two of the areas in which this expression is most conspicuous (one of which is particularly relevant to a broad understanding of law) are the concepts of time and power. Western cultures tend to express these concepts (as they tend to experience the world, generally) in *linear* terms. Time, for example, is conceived of having a beginning and, potentially, an end. People exist at a particular point upon a horizontally conceived timeline known as "history," and the only reality is the present, for the future has not yet happened and the past no longer exists. Power is a concept normally expressed in vertical terms; people exercise power "over" other people and things, or power is delegated "down" to other sources. The hierarchical image of power is a particularly crucial one for appreciating a Western concept of law from this sort of vertical perspective.

Eastern perceptions can be described, in contrast, as being *cyclical* in nature. Both time and power can be conceived as relative relationships that are shared, recurring, and not subject to such neat and simple experiences as two-dimensional Western conceptions might indicate. This conceptual approach will be evaluated more closely within the next chapter, but a rudimentary prelude to it should be offered, prior to continuing an evaluation of Western legal norms, as a way of appreciating this distinction. Therefore, an Eastern conception tends to emphasize the idea of time as a condition from which people seek, ultimately, to escape, rather than a line upon which people travel. Likewise, power is a shared phenomenon of a community, even though certain forces within that community appear to wield, at least superficially, greater power and prestige than other members. All members of the political community should strive to be, therefore, detached from a specific desire for a particular measure of this power, since it is, ultimately, shared by all. This idea (which will be developed more fully within the next chapter), contrasts markedly from the Western hierarchical approach, so its influence upon other social and political phenomenon is profound.

Another fundamental feature of Western thought is its tendency toward compartmentalization. Different, fundamental aspects of existence tend to exist within their own, self-contained categories. Western law, therefore, tends to be understood as a subject and practice that is distinct from other categories, including politics, economics, philosophy, and culture. Relationships may be acknowledged to exist among these categories, but the emphasis of analysis tends to favor parochial definitions and attitudes. Therefore, connections between law and other ideas and experiences (such as social, political, and philosophical relationships) may be acknowledged, but the distinctiveness of law from these other fields remains the dominant way of conceiving it.

By contrast, Eastern patterns of thought tend to emphasize the holistic relationship among various ideas and practices, so religion, politics, law, and philosophy do not appear to exist within exclusive categories but seem almost interchangeably, and intimately, interrelated. Again, this different perspective will receive greater emphasis within the next chapter, but this extremely brief introduction to it should provide a suitable contrast for grasping an appreciation of the very different pattern of Western thought and its influence upon an understanding of law.

It is, thus, possible to divide Western law into two broad traditions: natural law and positive law. While one of these traditions has emerged as dominant within the modern Western world, both of them have shaped a fundamental interpretation of the basic essence and purpose of law as it exists, today. Furthermore, even the non-dominant tradition continues to play a crucial role within the ongoing evolution of legal norms and practices. Therefore, it is critical to appreciate these two expansive categories before proceeding to more specific legal classifications and settings.

Origins of Natural Law

The natural law tradition usually is traced to the pre-Socratic period of ancient Greek civilization. Similar interpretations of, and approaches to, law can be discerned within other ancient Western civilizations. However, the ancient Greeks provided a comprehensive account of these legal ideas that established a foundation for the future development of this Western legal tradition, just as scholars traditionally have begun a survey of Western civilization with the communities of the Eastern Mediterranean region, particularly ancient Greek cultures.

Pre-Socratic Greek philosophers sought abstract models they could use for explaining all other phenomena. In terms of law (among other areas), they found that model through their observations of nature. They observed a nature that seemed to conform to certain uniform principles that perpetuated ultimate balance and stability. They believed that careful observation of the forces that guide nature could be imitated by the legal and political practices of the various Greek city-states, resulting in an equally stable, balanced, and relatively prosperous existence for them. Since the principles and rules that govern nature are observably uniform, a thematic imitation of those "natural" rules and principles should produce equally uniform laws and political practices, even among the numerous and diverse Greek city-states, as a model for the promotion of greater peace and unity of all their peoples.

But the observations of nature could be interpreted in profoundly different ways. Athenians might stress the equilibrium achieved among conflicting forces within nature, especially in terms of shifting climate, competing animals, and seasonal cycles, and conclude that laws which balance and accommodate the diverse forces and interests found among members of a city-state should, likewise, achieve balance and accommodation within the political institutions that these laws provide. Thus these "laws of nature" affirmed, for them, the superiority of the laws that organized and directed the workings of Athenian democracy. However, Spartans might stress the observation that competition among natural forces results in the ultimate survival and dominance of the strong, thus affirming the laws that guided and controlled Sparta's rigidly militaristic culture, with its harsh physical demands upon all of its citizens and non-citizens, alike. An ubiquitous law of nature that could surmount the divisions of ancient Greek city-states was frustratingly elusive.

Nonetheless, this search for a "natural" law provided a means of critically evaluating actual laws and practices and stimulate reforms and improvements. This natural law tradition began to achieve recognizable tenets that would form the basis for a relatively comprehensive approach to, and understanding of, law among Western civilizations. These tenets were relatively simple to identify, yet difficult to define with consensus, especially among scholars and leaders.

Essential Principles of Natural Law

The first principle of natural law is its aspiration to provide a universal standard of legal norms and structure. It is an abstract model; within its limits, varieties of expression may exist. Nonetheless, the law of nature imposes boundaries which all laws and legal practices that seek to be accepted as legitimate must not contravene. Therefore, if an interpretation of natural law demands conformity to an abstract notion of "balance," then all legal systems that seek its sanction must institute laws and legal practices that also promote this concept, such as Athenian legal provision for political institutions that mandate the active civic participation of all of important categories of Athenian citizenship, including aristocrats and common people, urban and rural dwellers, and all of the "tribal" divisions found within traditional Athenian culture.

This conformity was proposed as a way of evaluating not just the propriety of laws, but the extent to which they actually deserve to be recognized as laws, at all. A law that conforms to the abstract principles of natural law qualified as a "true" law, but a law that fails to adapt to those standards is not merely regarded as improper or flawed—it simply is treated as not being entitled to be regarded as a legitimate law in any meaningful sense. In that way, natural law has conferred a moral imperative upon law making and legal enforcement by creating these designations of "law" and "non-law" as substitutes for the more subjective labels of "good" and "bad" law. A statute, practice, or institution may bear a structural or procedural resemblance to law, but, if it fails to meet the theoretical standard of the natural law tradition, it is not a legitimate law and should be regarded, instead, as merely an unsanctioned political practice or, even, unjustified coercion.

The second principle of natural law is the belief that it is, complementary to its universal quality, a transhistorical tradition. Its principles are intended to remain valid, regardless of the passing of time. Changing conditions, throughout history, should not diminish their applicability. Therefore, natural law is regarded as being eternal. It is not subject to those conditions capable of changing, with time, everything else within the physical universe. This characteristic of natural law requires that it remain grounded upon abstract principles and relationships, rather than upon factors that are inspired by specific human experience. Specific circumstances may change, throughout history, but the theoretical assumptions of natural law that govern those circumstances and, indeed, even the disposition of change, itself, remain constant.

The two other fundamental principles of natural law are expressed in terms of philosophical mandates. The first mandate is described by the term *ontological*, which refers to a theory of "being," or a description of the fundamental quality of some central thing. All natural law emanates from a guiding, *ontological* expression, such as the ancient Greek emphasis upon legal norms that are consistent with the essence of nature. The *ontological* basis of natural law is found through an ability to define the fundamental character (indeed, the very "nature") of nature. That definition subsequently provides the abstract principles necessary for a law to qualify, truly, *as* a law.

The second mandate is described by the term *deontological*. Despite the similarity in their names, *deontological* is not the opposite of *ontological*; it refers, in fact, to an entirely different philosophical concept. The term *deontological* refers to a theory of "moral duty." It describes actions that must be taken in response to certain requirements or commandments. This mandate adds an important dimension to natural law, since it affects the way law is formulated and implemented. Laws that conform to the natural law do not merely establish limits, provide protections, or confer potential authority; they actually compel certain types of behavior.

Generally, the action mandated is derived from the *ontological* focus of a particular interpretation of natural law. Therefore, pre-Socratic Greek legal philosophers, who based their understanding of law upon the *ontological* definition of nature, further declared that valid laws direct the behavior of the city-states and their people to conform to this example of nature. Examples of this conformity include the laws that decreed the participation of all Athenian citizens in the conduct of their government. Holding office or serving on governmental bodies was not merely a condition that the law permitted; it was a moral duty that all citizens were compelled to fulfill. Otherwise, the sort of "balance" of forces within the community that the law of Athens promoted, as a reflection of the example of a "balanced" state of nature, could not be achieved.

Therefore, the *ontological* focus upon nature was supplemented by the *deontological* requirement of political participation. The fact that it was expressed within the context of an abstract model of nature that existed everywhere and remained historically constant combined with those features to complete this overall expression of a natural law. This abstract theory remained distinct from the specific laws of the various Greek city-states, but it established the criteria that would become increasingly accepted by both scholars and statesmen for evaluating the effectiveness, the moral propriety, and, even, the legitimacy, of any given legal statute or system.

Historical Development of Natural Law

These four theoretical characteristics of natural law (universal, transhistorical, *ontological*, and *deontological*) would remain essentially unchanged for thousands of years. However, the specific interpretation of natural law, especially its *ontological* focus, would evolve greatly through different periods and civilizations of Western history. Natural law would adapt its precepts to a changing world and, eventually, find a source of expression within areas of law and politics in which more conventional means of legal expression proved to be inadequate.

Later Greek philosophers would seek to refine the *ontological* basis of natural law. Plato would insist that this basis should be found within the "forms" of the ideal condition of existence, since physical things (including laws and the natural models which they seek to imitate) represent mere "shadows" of these perfect forms that include the concept of an ideal republic and the laws that govern it. His student, Aristotle, would reject this normative emphasis (which could be achieved only through the application of abstract reasoning) and propose, instead, an *ontological* emphasis grounded upon empirical observations of actual legal (including constitutional) institutions and practices, resting upon those features that work best, according to a critical assessment of physical evidence. Other Greek thinkers (including the Sophists and, later, the Stoics) adapted these approaches to their own desire to make distinctions between *physis* (the actual state of things) and *nomos* (the way things ought to be) within their critiques of law and politics, and these considerations served to guide attempts to implement and improve the legal and political status of the Greek city-states.

The Romans borrowed Greek ideas on natural law as a means for developing a legal structure that could be applicable to the varied cultures of their diverse empire. Roman legal scholars like Ulpian and Gaius sought to uncover common, or "universal," themes shared among these various peoples as a basis for a *jus naturale*, or "natural law," that Roman authorities could impose upon those relatively limited areas of governance that were considered particularly important to the security and prosperity of the Empire. The Christian accounts of the trial and execution of Jesus indicate this relationship: Roman officials were not interested in prosecuting Jesus for alleged religious crimes, leaving those matters to the discretion of the legal system of the local population, but when he was charged with a treasonous act against Roman authority (allegedly claiming to be a "king" and, thus, a rival to Caesar), those officials felt compelled to act.

This *jus naturale* formed the basis of a *jus gentium*, or "law of the peoples," addressing areas of political and economic concern that affected the empire as a whole. Other areas of local concern that were particular to a given culture and community could be addressed by native laws and customs, just as Roman citizens were governed by the *jus civile*, or "law of the city" of Rome, in recognition of the enduring fact that Rome remained, essentially, a city-state, with its own historic and culturally particular laws and customs applicable, uniquely, to its own citizens.

Still, this concept of an overarching natural law that could unite the imperial realm remained vague, despite the attempts of Byzantine scholars, commissioned by Emperor Justinian the Great, to codify a consistent legal system grounded, in part, upon a set of "universal" principles. However, the *ontological* and *deontological* basis for this system also remained vaguely rooted in an assumption of the superiority of Rome and its successors. The collapse of the Roman Empire and, eventually, its Byzantine successor state resulted in a fragmentation of political and legal authority and highly decentralized economic practices that prompted many people to want to recapture the unity and success of the ancient imperial period.

The enduring structural unity of the Roman Catholic Church, which had become the state religion of the late Western Roman Empire and paralleled its organizational structure, provided a focus for the continued understanding of law beyond the norms of local and tribal customs. Furthermore, the church and its scholars were able to apply the standards of natural law as a means of asserting the concept of a higher law that could unite all peoples, especially throughout Europe. The *ontological* source for this natural law came from the theological conception of a universe organized along hierarchical, static principles of order and authority. It is not a coincidence that these principles paralleled, and reinforced, the theoretical vision of the structure and authority of medieval European feudalism. This *ontological* vision promoted a *deontological* requirement of obedience to those sources of authority, since they emanated, ultimately (whether through the sacred authority of the system led by the Pope or the secular system led by the Holy Roman Emperor and various kings), from God. Furthermore, these precepts dictated all human activity, both in terms of requirements of feudal vassalage or the personal activities of human existence, including such matters as a requirement, among married couples, of biological reproduction.

These beliefs were regarded as being as universal and transhistorical as the religious beliefs that inspired them. They became systematized by scholarly authorities such as St. Thomas Aquinas, who categorized law into eternal, divine, natural, and human realms, with the natural law reflecting the eternal law that governs the physical universe and the direct commands of God provided by the divine law, and the human law being constrained by the limits imposed by this divine law. Theoretically, human laws that failed to conform to the guidance of the natural law did not qualify as law, and subjects of a sovereign authority that failed to be governed by natural law principles were, technically, released from their legal obligations.

Natural law was an attractive source for constructing a legal system for European civilizations that were seeking greater cohesion and expansion, including overseas. But the rise of the self-identifying nation-state undermined such universal pretensions, and an increasing belief that law should establish limits but not require any particular actions among people led to an eventual rejection of natural law as a basis for Western legal development. Nonetheless, natural law remained an important theoretical basis for understanding Western legal development. Hugo Grotius, the seventeenth century Dutch political theorist, adapted principles of natural law toward the establishment of a system of international law that could be universally accepted among states, imposing duties that these states were expected to fulfill through their relationships with each other, especially for maintaining international peace and stability. Still, natural law became largely displaced by the legal positivism that later will be described. However, its influence and significance has not disappeared, entirely.

The most meaningful use of natural law principles during the modern period has occurred within the development of a human rights tradition. This use is derived from an *ontological* emphasis upon the human condition as central to all legal ethics, a *deontological* insistence upon the moral duties that everyone (including states) must perform in relation to upholding human dignity, the belief (inspired by the humanism of the European Enlightenment) that the pursuit of human autonomy is the goal that universally binds all people and cultures, and the insistence that this human condition has been a consistent imperative throughout history. The most dramatic invocation of these principles occurred during the trials of war criminals, following World War II. Nazi officials who defended genocide and other actions by reference to their obedience to the laws of a sovereign German state were refuted by, and convicted as a result of, the declaration that a "higher" law overrode these statutes and orders. The Nuremberg Tribunal found this higher law to exist within "universal" principles of human dignity that not only forbade these sorts of crimes but also required officials, within reasonable bounds, to resist and, if possible, prevent them from happening. Nazi officials and other accused war crimes defendants who were punished under international law for these atrocities were found guilty, essentially, of contravening the *ontological* and *deontological* principles of a modern conception of a natural law that ultimately asserted its supremacy over domestic laws.

Despite the supplanting of natural law as a foundation for the Western legal tradition that emerged from Europe, it remains an important presence. The desire to establish moral justifications for legal actions maintains the attractiveness of natural law, in this respect. The demands of an increasingly integrated world, dominated by Western cultures, promotes a desire to find a universal source of legal norms and practices that all peoples can share. However, the significance of natural law has been clearly eclipsed by an alternative source of legal development that emerged from the overall changes that introduced the modern period of Western history.

Origins of Positive Law

The tradition of a "positive" law (also called legal positivism) rose in response to the profound changes that transformed a fragmented medieval Europe into its modern period. Perhaps, the change that most profoundly triggered this emergence was the rise of the European nation-state and its defining concept of sovereignty. The effective centralization of political power, the competition among nation-states, varying cultural sources of national identity (including customs, beliefs, and values) necessitated the development of instruments of consistent and functional legal institutions to express this development.

The emergence of the modern nation-state (largely in response to the development of centralized economic practices and principles associated with the rise of market systems) coincided with an increased emphasis upon rational explanations and justifications for all endeavors, including political activity. The intellectual focus of the European Enlightenment replaced a reliance upon faith and the teachings of authorities promoting an idea of universal principles with an appeal to human reason. This search for a rational basis of human ventures became expressed through the articulation of a "command theory" of law, especially as propounded by nineteenth-century commentators such as John Austin but, also, as asserted by a variety of legal scholars and political leaders since the beginning of the modern period of Western history, during the fifteenth and sixteenth centuries. This theory is based upon the belief that law is not defined by any recourse to higher norms or consistency with moral principles, but defined simply because it has been "commanded" by recognized sovereign authority.

Sovereignty is a condition of ultimate political power. A source of authority is recognized as being sovereign when it exercises political authority but is not subject to the authority of any other source of power. That sovereign authority can assume different guises: it can be a single monarch, an oligarchical association, or a democratic people. That authority can be delegated to another body or institution, such as a royal council or representative government. But it is the ability to recognize a source of power as actually being sovereign that makes possible the identification of law, since the legitimacy of the sovereign is measured by its effectiveness in imposing its legal will, rather than any impression of the moral propriety of that will.

Law does not qualify as law because it conforms to universal principles of morality; law qualifies as law because it enjoys the force of law. A law that violates moral principles may be perceived as a bad law, but it still qualifies as a law, unlike the natural law principle that immoral laws do not deserve to be considered law at all. It is this functional quality of the command theory of law that made it attractive for identifying legal norms, as well as an excellent tool for promoting the sovereign goals of a nation-state. It also conforms to the intellectual practices that emerged from the rise of the modern period.

Historical Development of Positive Law

The scientific revolution of the seventeenth and eighteenth centuries spurred an enduring desire to establish all human activity upon the basis of demonstrable facts and observations rather than the speculative tendencies of previous ideas and practices. According to this approach, law should not be derived from unprovable moral conjecture but from empirically experienced sources that can be revealed to be valid through its actual, effective application. Since this approach to law depends upon its observable, institutional qualities, it is described as being "positive." Furthermore, this empirical emphasis also tends to invoke an expectation that law can be reduced to rational norms and procedures that, like the scientific method, can be categorized, classified, measured, and applied in a systematic, consistent, and, even, predictable way.

Legal positivism emerged as an approach to law that is dominated by a desire to achieve a precise process, consistent language, and uniformity. This desire has led to a tendency to insist upon a rational basis for all expressions and evaluations of law. Such an approach was embraced by many scholars and legal practitioners because it could be applied, in a neutral fashion, to any society, regardless of its culture, beliefs, or fundamental principles. The content of law can vary under the norms of legal positivism; it is the rational structure that frames those differing articulations of specific statutes, rules, and procedures which remains constant and rationally identifiable. This approach prompted the belief that law could be expressed "objectively," since its substance remains irrelevant to its legitimacy. This claim is an expression of the fact that each society can invest its legal system with any subjective source of beliefs and values. It also is a conscious rejection of supposed claims to "universal" legal principles that its critics claim to be the attempt of self-proclaimed moral authorities to impose their will against the will of the sovereign—including a democratic polity.

The goal of upholding an emerging popular sovereign will against non-sovereign sources that might want to manipulate or suppress that democratic will spurred strong, rationalistic defenses of legal positivism. The most prominent of these defenses emerged from the eighteenth-century philosophical reformers known as utilitarians. Led by eminent scholars such as James Mill and Jeremy Bentham, the utilitarians sought to promote political and legal reform by overcoming prejudices and uncritical acceptance of traditional beliefs and practices through logical and empirical processes. This approach resulted in the development of a principle of "utility" that measured the appropriateness of an action or institution upon the basis of its practical ability to promote human happiness, rather than its conformity to any abstract moral standard.

Utilitarian thought reduced all human activity to a logically determined desire to seek pleasure and avoid pain. This pain/pleasure dichotomy could be applied toward an evaluation of all human activity, especially when it concerned the exercise of sovereign authority. These motives are tangible, measurable, and, arguably, shared by all people, so they are not subject to competing explanations of ethical standards. Therefore, laws that promote "pleasure" and prevent "pain" are preferable because they match this empirically measured reality. These laws should be enacted and enforced, ideally, from an unemotional, neutral perspective.

A student of Mill and Bentham, John Austin, applied this theory of utility to the understanding of law. He emphasized an approach that grounded the law upon broad principles that could be segmented into more narrow, derivative categories that remain, nonetheless, consistent with these more fundamental ideas and practices. Different classifications of law can be developed to address different political, social, and economic matters, but they remain subject to rules of logic and consistent criteria of analysis, interpretation, and application. Austin thus sought to make law "scientific" and permanently subject to value-neutral standards. This nineteenth-century emphasis upon a systematized legal structure that can adapt to any set of policies, goals, or values, without making moral judgments, has come to characterize modern legal expectations and practices, particularly among Western countries. It became bolstered by interpretive movements such as legal realism (inspired by the broader realist movement that, especially within the arts, stressed "real" reflections of human society over idealized portrayals), which also sought to gauge laws according to practical results, rather than normative preferences.

Legal positivism defined law in a parochial manner by providing specific criteria for identifying it. Therefore, a clear distinction was made between matters that are relevant to law and matters that lie beyond the law. Prior to the development of this clear distinction, law could provide a way of defining and regulating all aspects of human life and activity. Positive law made possible the modern distinction between public matters, which the law addresses, and private matters, which law does not regulate. It helped to promote an image of human freedom and the proper role of government which enhanced its reputation as the most appropriate model of legal development.

However, the atrocities of the twentieth century, especially during the Second World War, led to a reevaluation of the propriety of legal positivism as a strictly neutral approach to law. A strong desire to renew the relationship between law and appeals to a higher moral standard often created a sentiment that traditional legal positivism suffers from a certain paucity of human values that gives the law its ultimate legitimacy. This image often has exposed legal positivism to a charge that it is cold, calculating, and tolerant of abuses and atrocities that undermine the ultimate purposes and aspirations of the law. Therefore, increasing attempts to draft international legal norms that conform to globally agreed principles of morals and values have characterized many of the scholarly and practical approaches to legal development of the twenty-first century.

Both the natural law and positive law traditions have shaped the ongoing evolution of Western legal norms and institutions, with legal positivism often shaping the behavior of legal practitioners and natural law often directing the legal motives of politicians, legal scholars, and many of the people who are subject to, and beneficiaries of, law. Constitutions frequently become the platform for attempts to reconcile these traditions, particularly in terms of articulating political and philosophical goals within the institutional framework of practical legal institutions. But all areas of Western law remain subject to the ongoing influence of both natural law and legal positivism.

References

St. Thomas Aquinas, *Summa Theologiæ*, Thomas Gilby and T. C. O'Brien, trans. and eds. Cambridge, Blackfriars, 1966.

John Austin, *Lectures on Jurisprudence*, Robert Campbell, ed. London, John Murray, 1885.

Jeremy Bentham, *The Works of Jeremy Bentham*, John Bowring, ed. Edinburgh, William Tait, 1843.

Ronald Dworkin, *Law's Empire*. Cambridge, MA, Harvard University Press, 1986.

Gaius, *The Institutes of Gaius*, William M. Gordon and O. F. Robinson, trans. and ed. Ithaca, NY, Cornell University Press, 1988.

Wesley Newcombe Hohfeld, *Fundamental Legal Conceptions*, Walter Wheeler Cook, ed. New Haven, CT, Yale University Press, 1964.

Harold J. Laski, *Authority in the Modern State*. Hamden, CT, Archon, 1968.

Charles de Secondat, Baron de Montesquieu, *L'esprit des lois*. Paris: Librarie Médici, 1948.

Heinrich Rommen, *The Natural Law: A Study in Legal and Social History and Philosophy*, Thomas R. Hanley, trans. St. Louis, Herder, 1959.

Lloyd L. Weinreb, *Natural Law and Justice*. Cambridge, MA, Harvard University Press, 1987.

CHAPTER 3

Eastern Legal Heritage

Eastern Perspectives of the World

Unlike Western cultures, Eastern civilizations often have stressed an interrelationship among all human endeavors. This holistic approach can make it difficult to identify a clearly defined category of "Eastern law" that is distinct from politics, philosophy, religion, or other social and economic areas of life. According to a conventional Western approach, politics, economics, sociology, psychology, religion, art, and other endeavors may interact, but they are treated, nonetheless, as being separate entities which are comprehended, properly, in isolation from each other. The Western tradition compartmentalizes the various facets of human existence and interaction. Strict distinctions are made among different activities, institutions, patterns of thought, and intellectual disciplines. The experiences of many Eastern cultures are profoundly different. Therefore, it is crucial to identify the broad abstraction of a culturally Eastern "worldview" before the notion of an Eastern approach to law can be effectively addressed.

Western cultural and intellectual perspectives can be described as "linear," while it is possible to describe Eastern cultural and intellectual perspectives as being "cyclical" in nature. Law, in this sense, describes a way of providing order to relationships that are shared, recurring, and not subject to such neat and simple experiences as the limiting or controlling role that Western articulations of law generally indicate. Law remains an expression of political power for Eastern communities. However, power is treated as a shared phenomenon of those communities. Certain parties within that community may appear to exercise greater power and prestige than other members. But the ultimate belief of political power as a shared commodity provides a very profound, though subtle, source of legal norms and practices among these cultures.

Likewise, some Eastern traditions contend that time is a recurring state of existence that humans seek to escape through the attainment of enlightenment. Time does not exist as a separate component of existence; it is interwoven into a larger "fabric." Again, the concept of power is perceived in a similar manner. Political authority is not, strictly speaking, something that is imposed from above, nor is it something that is exercised *over* other people. Law, as an expression of political authority, assists in the ultimate expression of sovereign authority, rather than imposing the will of the sovereign upon the community. This idea contrasts markedly from the Western hierarchical approach. It is a distinction that can be appreciated most clearly through an evaluation of certain prominent philosophical traditions that are most relevant for gaining this Eastern understanding of law, especially among prominent Asian countries such as China, India, Japan, and other civilizations.

Confucianism and Law

Arguably, the most prominent of all Eastern cultural traditions and systems of thought and expression is Confucianism. Its values and explanation of the cultural and political life of many Asian communities has had a profound influence for 2,500 years. It dominated China as an officially sanctioned political philosophy throughout most of China's imperial history. Even the official denunciation of Confucianism by the Chinese Communist Party has not diminished its significance for understanding the underlying principles of law and politics in contemporary China. Therefore, an appreciation of this self-consciously political philosophical tradition is vital for gaining a meaningful comprehension of law within Eastern cultures.

Kung Fu-tse was an itinerant teacher and government official during the very tumultuous period of the Chou dynasty (during the fifth century BCE, according to the Western calendar), in which imperial authority was effectively displaced by warring, feudal states that fostered instability and undermined security and prosperity. Kung Fu-tse, or, as he his better known in the West, Confucius (a Latin transcription of this name, later provided by Jesuit scholars), offered a way for these military and political leaders, and the people they ruled, to adapt traditional patterns of thought and existence to their lives and the disposition of their communities that could overcome the chaos and meagerness that the current turmoil inflicted. His teachings reflected principles and experiences already accepted by many people in China, so his formal ideas became dominant throughout this part of the world, relatively quickly.

Confucius stressed many principles; certain of these ideals seem particularly relevant to an Eastern understanding of law. An overarching concept is the ideal of "harmony." This concept differs from a more parochial image of "balance," since it is not directed towards forces or interests in opposition to each other.

Instead, harmony stresses the interconnectedness and interdependence of all members of the community. All separate needs are legitimate, but they cannot be pursued in isolation, nor should they be sought to the detriment of other needs and interests. A good illustration of this principle is the relationship between humans and nature. Humans need natural resources for their survival and comfort, yet the exploitation of these resources will result in a diminishing of their future availability and destruction of the environment that generates them. Likewise, humans who receive a paucity of these resources will be unable to thrive or, even, survive. Since nature remains relatively constant, humans must learn to foster an ongoing relationship that both preserves the growth and stability of nature while extracting those resources they legitimately require.

Similar relationships exist within a political community. A harmonious relationship among all of the interests within a community must be maintained, for the exploitation and destruction of any of them will, ultimately, diminish the whole. Conciliation and consensus are, therefore, far preferable to the imposition of the will of any one part of the community, whether it be a single ruler, a powerful faction, or even a majority of all the people. The exclusion of the needs and interests of any part of the community will lead to its diminishment and, consequently, its inability to contribute effectively to the prosperity of the whole.

Arguably, the most important legal concept for promoting this central principle of harmony is the notion of *gîri*, which translates roughly as "mutual obligation" or "reciprocal duty." This concept belies a popular image of simple obedience to a paternal ruler that often is associated with Confucianism, for, under this concept of *gîri*, a ruler owes duties to the subjects as surely as subjects owe duties to a ruler. This concept underscores the interrelated and interdependent nature of the community and it directs legal relationships to reinforce these duties. A good illustration of this correlation is the sense of *gîri* that is practiced between peasants and soldiers. Peasants have a duty to support soldiers, especially in terms of providing food for their sustenance. Soldiers have a reciprocal duty to support peasants by protecting them from attack. Peasants who fail to perform their duty contribute to the weakening of the soldiers, undermining their own security through the maintenance of well-fed and, thus, truly effective protectors. Likewise, soldiers who abuse peasants contribute to the inability of these peasants to be fully productive in producing food, undermining their own effectiveness through the potential loss of nourishment needed for sustaining an effective fighting force.

The relationship between subjects and rulers also conforms to this expectation and helps to define their legal relationship under a Confucian ethic. Subjects who refuse to obey and support their rulers contribute to instability and chaos, ultimately undermining the conditions they need for security and prosperity. Likewise, rulers who exploit their subjects will weaken them to the extent that they are unable to generate the overall productivity that provides the basis for the rulers' own resources, as well as an unwillingness of these subjects to support their rulers in time of crisis. This relationship is directed by an understanding of *giri* that is expressed in terms of legal arrangements that seek to coordinate the needs of all parts of the community, for the benefit and, consequently, harmony of the whole.

This idea contrasts sharply with Western perceptions of legal relationships based upon mistrust, a need to control, and a deemphasis upon the concept of obligation in favor of limits and realms of permitted action. The spheres of public and private are far less relevant to a Confucian conception of law than they are to modern Western legal ideas. This Confucian ideal is expressed by the term *li*, which roughly translates as "law" but expresses a meaning that is more subtle and profound than the Western term, and its association with rigid rules, often conveys. *Li* reflects a concept of correct legal conduct that is based upon the guidance of *giri*. It is a guiding principle, rather than a set of rules or specific commands.

Li, in fact, underscores a perception of law that rejects the abstract rules, structures, and institutions that characterize Western legal systems. This formal image of Western law often is regarded with suspicion, since it can be manipulated on behalf of the selfish interest of the party that is providing and interpreting the law. Furthermore, formal approaches to law can undermine its flexibility, making it impossible to respond to changing circumstances while maintaining the harmonious spirit that the law is intended to convey. *Li* is grounded upon a willingness to make all actions conform to broadly understood beliefs and principles. Therefore, rulers who are influenced by this philosophical approach tend to abstain from the imposition of specific legal procedures, edicts, and prohibitions, relying, instead, upon shared measurements of the true, holistic purpose of legal relationships and their proper conduct as a guide for all members of the community.

Confucius suggested that one of the ways that a community can be guided toward a meaningful appreciation of *giri* and *li* is through ritual. The intricacies of dance, music, and other actions involving, potentially, large numbers of people reinforce a broader ideal of harmony that also was augmented, in ancient China, by court ritual. Each participant within this sort of activity has a specific role, and an inability to perform that role according to the precise guidance of its master can ruin the overall effect, thus diminishing the whole. Court ritual was used to emphasize essential relationships among people and the fact that these relationships are not one-dimensional. This emphasis could be both symbolic and functional, and it can be replicated through other public actions and institutions, including legal tribunals and their procedures.

The "ceremony" of a trial, for example, might seem, under certain circumstances, redundant or superfluous, but it also serves a purpose for the entire community by reiterating these relationships, including the obligations that the accused persons do, or should, owe to the judges, the community, their families, and themselves. Judges play a particularly important role by serving as the "instructors" of these reciprocal duties through their interpretation and application of the law. They play a role that is similar to the dance master or music conductor, for they are a focal point for guiding all activities into a harmonious whole.

This role of the "teacher" became politically important among Eastern cultures. Confucius served as the paramount model of that role. He sought to instruct both rulers and subjects; he expected these rulers and subjects both to reciprocate his duty to provide the benefit of his wisdom by allowing themselves to be guided by that wisdom. This role became the basis for the civil servants who dominated China's political and legal existence until the twentieth century. Indeed, these mandarins were required to pass examinations in Confucian thought in order to qualify for these lucrative positions. More recently, the role of other Chinese public authorities, including legal officials, continues to reflect this ideal, and all other members of the community have a duty to be guided legally in this way, just as these officials have a duty to provide good guidance, in accordance with their expertise and for the harmonious benefit of the whole community.

The influence of these Confucian principles transcends the dominance of Confucianism as a formally acknowledged doctrine. Principles of harmony, *giri*, *li*, ritual, and other ideals continue to be reflected, in other guises, among many modern Eastern communities. It is consistent with overall observations concerning Eastern, as opposed to Western, patterns of thought and perception. It is, possibly, the most influential of these traditions, but it is not the only one.

Legalism and Law

The most influential interpretation of Confucian thought was reinforced through the teachings of Confucius' most prominent disciple, Mencius. However, these teachings were manipulated, especially during the second century BCE, to conform to the practical needs of leaders who sought to rationalize their autocratic use of political power. The most prominent advocate of this interpretation was Han Fei-tzû, and he provided a basis for the political theory that came to be known as

Legalism. This doctrine emphasized the formulation of positive laws that would dictate the duties of all subjects. They would be required to obey these laws, without challenge, and they would provide strict guidance for all subjects of the government. These laws would be regarded as permanent and inviolable, so they could not be subjected to interpretations that would seek to harmonize them with a broader spirit of the community.

The ruler would be the sole authority for interpreting the law, defining the spirit of the community, and establishing the criteria for maintaining harmony. The emphasis rested upon a sense of imposed order, so the need for specific laws that subjects could read, understand, and obey was paramount. Although stress was placed upon positive laws, rather than teachers, councillors, or other people who would provide the guidance of *li*, the result was to bolster the absolute power of the ruler, under the guise of a reinterpretation of the Confucian ideal of reverence for paternalistic authority.

Indeed, the Confucian concept of *li*, which refers to behavior that is "lawful" in the sense that it conforms to the harmony promoted by *giri*, is displaced, under Legalist doctrine, with a concept of *fa*. This term also roughly translates as "law," but its more precise meaning conveys a sense of "force," rather than a guiding principle. It refers to an underscored political goal of using law as an instrument of obedience. It is intended to ensure stability through servility, which becomes the primary purpose of an autocratic regime and can be mistaken for a sense of harmony, particularly by a population that has experienced the destablizing effects of violence, disorder, and uncertainty that generally accompany the struggles for power that precede the establishment of such rulers (or the maintenance of their dynastic claims in opposition to political challenge or military rebellion) and the regimes they wish to perpetuate.

These imposed values become a new standard of "harmony." They may be accepted by the community, but they tend not to be inclusive and, thus, not truly holistic, either. Legalism has not enjoyed general success as an alternative interpretation of the sort of beliefs and values articulated by Confucianism, especially as received through the school of thought established by Mencius. Yet, as a legal and political rationalization, it has persisted as a doctrine cited by political authorities in defense of laws and actions that appear to be arbitrary, capricious, and, even, brutal. Political leaders who dismiss criticism of their regimes, especially Western criticism, often claim that their actions are consistent with the fundamental beliefs and values of Eastern cultures, especially in accordance with the tradition of Confucius. However, their actions often truly reflect the rationalizations of

Legalist doctrine, which usually represents an oversimplification and, even, perversion of these more widely held beliefs and values.

Taoism and Law

Taoism is a practice of perceiving existence that stresses the interconnectedness of all forces. The word *tao* refers to the idea of a "path," and it is the desire to conform to the mentoring of this path, rather than a resistance to it in search of separate goals, that can lead to human happiness. Taoism is a philosophical system that tends to focus upon personal development and relationships, but it offers instruction that can be applied to all aspects of existence, including law.

Lao Tzu, The fifth-century BCE spiritual leader and political counselor, is credited, by tradition, with the establishment of a comprehensive explanation of Taoist principles. The central symbol of Taoism, the circle representing the different forces of *yin* and *yang*, provides a visual example of its central tenets. Seemingly opposite forces are not really in opposition to each other, since one force relies upon the other for its very existence. The true path is to appreciate this complementary relationship of all things and use it as a model for one's own life and the principles that govern a community. The concept of "day" would be meaningless if "night" did not also exist, since day is actually defined by its quality of being different from night. Otherwise, the condition called "day" would simply be a static state, indistinguishable from anything else because of a lack of contrast. Furthermore, in a physical sense, unremitting daylight, despite the superficial impression of its superior qualities among octurnal creatures, would prove detrimental to health and sanity without the cyclical effect that a period of darkness provides living creatures.

Likewise, all things achieve their true meaning through this contrast and, as a result, find peace and fulfillment. This analogy can be extended to all fields of human endeavor, which remain interconnected. The ability to harmonize these contrasting forces, rather than destroy seemingly conflicting opposites, is necessary for attaining this state of fulfillment. Politically and legally, for example, the ability to reconcile divergent policies, rules, and goals that permit all parties to achieve their true purpose is the result of finding and pursuing the *tao*. When Japan was first exposed to Western interests, the immediate reaction of its leaders and people was to resist these seemingly antithetical forces. However, during the late nineteenth century, Japanese political leaders determined that a more useful path would be to embrace these foreign ways by blending their beneficial aspects with the practices and principles of a traditionally Eastern Japanese culture. Arguably, the result of this reconciliation of "opposites" was the emergence of a modern, successful country that was capable of achieving great prosperity.

A central source for addressing this ideal can be found in the *Tao Te Ching*, which is a book, attributed to Lao Tzu, that offers guidance, through representative symbols, for finding the path and reconciling oppositional forces. It is not a specific guide to conventional activities of a political or legal community. However, from the Taoist approach, it is possible to observe certain ideals and practices that have, apparently, influenced the legal development of certain Eastern communities. Many Asian corporations, for example, have adopted an organizational technique that rejects the Western tendency to regard workers and management as competing opponents and, instead, seeks to reconcile the goals of each part of the corporate body into a cohesive whole.

Corporate policy, for example, often is not imposed by the board of directors upon the organization but is subject, instead, to the input and amendments of every one of its sectors. The result often is a policy that enjoys the genuine support of all, even if no separate interest achieves its complete goals. The role of government within the business sector often follows a similar model, with government officials seeking to reconcile the broader, often different interests of labor and industry by creating a holistic response to the relationship and guiding these interests toward a concordance that benefits society, as a whole, according to the overall vision of the government.

Since the *tao* is a guide, and not a definitive set of ideals or beliefs, it is receptive to the influence of other systems of thought and perception. The influence of Confucianism and Buddhism often are evident within communities that have been shaped by Taoism. In this way, it is possible for Taoist principles to find effective expression within more conventional areas of public life, including laws and methods of legal interpretation. The legal relationship of the "benefactor," the motivating concept of "shame" (especially in contrast to the Western concept of "sin"), and the desire to resolve legal disputes in a manner that is most beneficial to the whole community, are aspects of this influence, also found within other traditions influenced by this ideal, such as Japanese Shintoism. Therefore, it is important to avoid minimizing the general contribution of Taoism to the Eastern influence upon legal thought and practice, despite its apparent subtleties.

Hinduism and Law

Although it is more conventionally regarded as the most dominant religion of India, Hinduism reflects the holistic tendencies of Eastern thought, in general, through its influence over all aspects of the lives of people and their respective communities. Hinduism offers a perspective upon law and legal relationships that is critical for understanding the shaping of legal norms throughout south-central Asia. It is particularly effective, in this respect, through its ability to explain and order social relationships which the law, ultimately, reinforces.

Hinduism conceives of humanity as an abstraction that seeks ultimate union with a greater cosmos. Humans can find happiness only by being released from the limits of the physical world and achieving oneness with the universal *ohm*, which serves as a representation of that force which is the essence of all things. Hinduism offers knowledge of human limitation and a means for achieving the dispassionate detachment from the things of this world that will make this spiritual fulfillment attainable. Various representations of the infinite are found within numerous gods (actually different incarnations of the same god-force) that offer this guidance. It also is provided within sacred writings (such as the *Vedic* scriptures) and their interpretations, especially as offered by people particularly designated for that responsibility.

The most important Hindu concept for understanding its more particular influence upon the law is the principle of *dharma*. Its rough translation from Hindi is "duty," but it also can be interpreted as meaning "lawful." It encompasses the customs and practices that all people are expected to observe, especially in terms of their relationships with each other. It identifies behavior that is based upon a person's status, as determined by birth, rather than attempting to define human happiness through individual or, even, collective preferences.

A variety of significant treatises on *dharma* have been provided by traditional authorities. Collectively, they are known as the *dharmasastras*, and they address a wide range of subject areas, often in verse, that provide guidance for people according to their caste status. The vagaries and contradictions that arise among the various *dharmasastras* are clarified within additional works known as the *nibandhas*, and these works, collectively, provide a key for understanding relationships among Hindu people, especially in terms of their caste identities. Four main castes are divided into thousands of subcastes; these four main castes segment a community according to the primary role of the people who belong to each of them.

Castes are dominated by customary rules that are enforced primarily through the informal pressure of common ties to each caste identity. The four main castes include the *brahmin* (spiritual and intellectual leaders), *kshattriya* (military personnel and civil authorities), *vaisyas* (merchants, artisans, and entrepreneurs), and *sudras* (general laborers and servants), with an additional category of "outcastes," or "untouchables," who have no formal caste status (often owing to a violation of *dharma* resulting in a loss of caste status) and exist at the economic and social periphery of the Hindu community. The conformity of members of a caste to the guidance of *dharma* can improve them and their future status (during the next phase of their cyclical worldly existence) or, possibly, release them from the ongoing cycle of physical existence, and the inevitable grief and suffering that results from it, and attainment of a state of *nirvana*, through which union with the universal *ohm* is achieved.

The rejection of all desire is the key to the attainment of *nirvana*. This condition cannot be achieved through the cultivation of human motivations; it can be achieved only through dispassionate pursuit of the duties ascribed to persons in accordance with their caste status. *Dharma*, therefore, provides guidance for attaining this purpose. It serves, in that sense, as "law" that provides a *deontological* imperative. The interpretation of the requirements imposed by *dharma* can be modified, according to the needs or conditions of the community and its people, but the lack of personal motive must remain paramount. Guidance for that purpose is provided for each community through the *panchayat*, or body of elders who come, ordinarily, from the *brahmin* caste. It also can be applied toward an interpretation of civil legal norms and customs, although the relationship between *dharma* and the specific political and legal activities of the physical world generally is not formalized or, even, officially acknowledged.

Secular legal authorities are bound by the laws that are promulgated for their community, but they may apply the principles of *dharma* for their application to various circumstances. People who have committed crimes identified under these civic laws should be convicted and punished, but jurists who are influenced by Hindu beliefs and values may determine that mitigating circumstances exist for someone whose reason for committing the crime stems from *dharma*. Tales of men who have murdered their daughters to prevent them from marrying outside their caste and are punished with a relatively brief prison sentence provide a commonly reported example of this approach. Since they were not motivated by greed, anger, hatred, or other malice but simply were attempting to conform to the duties that this "higher law" directs through the *dharmasastras* and *nibandhas*, civil authorities have been willing to use this matter of motive as a factor for justifying a lenient sentence. Although objections from the wider community, including non-Hindus, may deter the frequency of this inclination, it remains an example of the enduring influence that Hindu beliefs can convey to the legal norms of a modern civil society.

The distinction between religious guidance and secular authority is a feature of communities dominated by Hinduism. However, the degree of discernment remains vague, particularly in terms of the interpretation of legal norms and practices. Legislation and civil legal rules and practices exist within a separate realm, called *artha*, which consists of commands, imposed by a secular ruler, that subjects are bound to obey but which remain distinct from the guidance of *dharma*. Nonetheless, it is impossible to separate completely the relationship of one from the other, making the effect of Hindu beliefs and values particularly important for the purpose of truly understanding the concept of law, including at the constitutional level, among these cultural communities.

Legally Comparing East and West

This overview of select traditions of Eastern thought, and its relationship to the idea of law, is necessarily brief and incomplete. However, even a perfunctory introduction to these patterns of perception and reaction, though potentially oversimplified, needs to be presented, especially to a Western audience. Western observers frequently find examinations of legal matters confusing when placed within the context of Eastern civilizations.

These civilizations are as diverse as their Western counterparts, yet they exhibit similar patterns of expression that prompt similar responses to the general concept of law. The non-hierarchical tendency of comprehending political and legal power, the lack of distinction among various fields of human life and activity, the interrelationship of personal and social existence, provide dynamic responses to this idea of law, even though Western observers might find them frustratingly subtle. Nonetheless, it remains intensely crucial to understand and appreciate them; otherwise, the comparison of the legal realms of these communities can be grossly oversimplified and, subsequently, badly misunderstood.

References

John H. Berthrong and Evelyn Berthrong, *Confucianism: A Short Introduction*. Oxford, Oneworld, 2000.
John Eaton Calthorpe Blofeld, *Taoism: The Road to Immortality*. Boston, Shambhala, 2000.
J. L. Brockington, *The Sacred Thread: Hinduism in Its Continuity and Diversity*. Edinburgh, University of Edinburgh Press, 1996.
Masaji Chiba, ed., *Asian Indigenous Law: Its Interaction with Received Law*. London, KPI, 1986.
Chin Kim, *Selected Writings on Asian Law*, Littleton, CO, Rothman, 1982.
Honghe Liu, *Confucianism in the Eyes of a Confucian Liberal: Hsu Fu-kuan's Critical Examination of the Confucian Legal Tradition*. New York, Peter Lang, 2001.
Brian E. McKnight, ed., *Law and the State in Traditional East Asian Law*. Honolulu, University of Hawaii Press, 1987.
John K. Nelson, *Enduring Identities: The Guise of Shinto in Contemporary Japan*. Honolulu, University of Hawaii Press, 2000.
Leslie Palmier, ed., *State and Law in Eastern Asia*. Brookfield, VT, Dartmouth Publishing, 1996.
A. K. Pavithran, *Substance of Public International Law*. Madras, Rajendran, 1965.
Isabelle Robinet, *Taoism: Growth of a Religion*, Phyllis Brooks, trans. Stanford, CA, Stanford University Press, 1997.
Poh-Ling Tang, ed., *Asian Legal Systems: Society and Pluralism in East Asia*. Sydney, Butterworths, 1997.
Max Weber, *The Religion of India: The Sociology of Hinduism and Buddhism*, Hans H. Gerth and Don Martindale, trans. and ed. New Delhi, Munshiram Manoharlal, 1992.
Hsin-chung Yao, *An Introduction to Confucianism*. Cambridge, Cambridge University Press, 2000.

CHAPTER 4

Ideology and Law

Law as Ideological Expression

The fact that the formal concept of a public law arose at the same time as the emergence of modern ideologies is not coincidental. Both developments occurred in response to fundamental changes in the nature of Western civilizations, particularly in terms of the advent of the modern society. Constitutions, as the most conspicuous instrument of public law, are, essentially, philosophical documents, and the dominant role of ideology, particularly throughout the Western world, must be addressed in order to appreciate the true nature, purpose, and effect of contemporary law, particularly from a comparative perspective. Despite misunderstood claims of "objectivity," modern Western law is as ideologically driven as any other political institution.

Law is a reflection of a political will. That reflected political will is, in turn, an expression of economic conditions and desires that are the culmination of the human quest for survival and prosperity. An ideology offers a conceptual justification of that economic reality through the promotion of supportive principles, values, norms, and the institutions that emanate from the emergence of these forces. This theme of development follows a familiar pattern: underlying technological and environmental shifts (both natural and social) alter human economic behavior; people reassess and adjust their beliefs and values to conform to this new economic deportment; political institutions are altered or created in response to, and in support of, this economic activity; philosophers and political theorists articulate the beliefs and values that explain and justify these institutions within an abstract, comprehensive, theoretical framework that (within the modern Western tradition, in particular) is called an ideology. René Descartes, the sixteenth-century philosopher, helped to provide an explanation of this concept of ideology, as distinct from other philosophical constructs, in terms of its necessity for identifying and labeling the social, political, and economic phenomena that combined to create the equally modern concept of a "society." The fact that heterogeneous political communities could unite disparate peoples into a socially cohesive habitat demanded the adoption of a "study" of the "ideas" (the Greek translation of these concepts being *logos* and *idea*, from which the word "ideology" is derived) that allowed people to identify, and make sense of, the functional features of this society that united them.

The institutional response to this pattern of technological, economic, and political transformations that implements all other institutional change and expresses, most forcefully, these ideological constructs is the law. Many modern legal practitioners may be derisive of this attitude, consistent with the value-neutral assumptions and "scientific" aspirations of contemporary legal positivism. However, the denial of an essential, defining relationship between ideology and law is an invitation to an elementally flawed interpretation, especially from the perspective of public law and the political purposes that law ultimately serves. This relationship between ideology and law is, therefore, particularly pivotal for achieving a meaningful comprehension of law.

Medieval European Antecedents of Legal Norms and Values

The previous chapter, addressing natural law, illustrated the relationship between an *ontological* definition of law and the social, religious, economic, and political conditions that have shaped it. The collapse of the Roman Empire in the West, the tribal invasions and migrations that preceded and followed that disintegration, and the decentralization of political and economic life that resulted from these events prompted the development of a localized, agrarian economic system. This development produced an economic order that was labor intensive, precarious, and dependent upon the control of land and the extraction of its resources.

Rome's centralized legal structure was displaced by the tribal legal traditions and local customs of the myriad of agrarian communities that succeeded the former unity of Western Europe. The dependence placed upon a population dedicated to this labor-intensive economic system prompted the formulation of a complex image of a rigidly hierarchical political order, reinforced by the continued institutional presence of an equally hierarchical Christian presence, throughout Europe, that justified its organizational principles by reference to a theological construct of an equally hierarchical, ordered, and static universe under the ultimate control of God. Sources of centralized political authority did, indeed, exist, especially in the form of kings and, theoretically, a Holy Roman Emperor placed in authority over all of them. The presence of this hierarchy was crucial for justifying the imposed order that guaranteed a relatively immobile population dedicated to agricultural production and other, directly supportive economic activities. But the reality was that effective control could not be maintained from such a central position, so it was the more local sources of political authority, in the form of the lower nobility, that was the true source of effective power throughout the medieval period.

A tiny percentage of the population controlled, through its domination of the land, the rest of the population, with a slightly larger military force supplied for the purpose of guaranteeing some form of compliance, order, and stability. This condition was expressed politically through the emergence of the feudal system of vassal relationships, in which an overlord granted a vassal exclusive use of a portion of land (but not, technically, outright ownership) in exchange for personal loyalty, economic and military support, and a pledge to maintain this system. Therefore, the values of most people of this period (extending roughly from the sixth through the fifteenth centuries) came to vindicate this situation, since it was the only condition they could readily conceive.

These values included, in addition to an image of hierarchical authority and a *deontological* requirement to obey that authority in all things, a personal identity that is inextricably tied to one's rank and station within the larger hierarchical system, the strict stratification of the community and the constraint to accept one's station (as determined by birth) and fulfill its expectations and obligations, and a sense of identity that emanates from the perception of belonging to a broader, mechanistic system, whether defined in terms of the feudal system, the church, or the abstract universe. The legal expression of this value system described the feudal order. Specific manifestations of this legal expression rested upon local customs, but the theory of a natural law that served as a higher legal ideal helped to preserve a sense of uniformity among these variations.

An example of these legal trends are revealed through the laws that sought to reenforce socio-economic status and relationships. Practically all regions of the continent, for example, maintained variations of the "sumptuary laws," which dictated the quality of food, clothing, shelter, entertainment, and other features of each person's life, depending upon their social rank. The local version of this law might vary in some particulars, but its general purpose conformed to the natural law expectation to conform to the *ontological* disposition of God's universe and the *deontological* requirement of fulfilling the obligations and necessary social relationships that one's social and economic status demanded.

Important technological changes, beginning around the fourteenth century, altered the basis of this medieval economy. Gradually, the quantity of agrarian production could be increased, greatly, with less effort. Increases in population, and a need to find alternative means for the economic support of that surplus population, coincided with an increase in prosperity that created a desire for goods beyond the things necessary for mere survival. The towns grew in size and importance as displaced peasants sought an alternative means of support by becoming apprenticed to guilds and learning a trade, while increased prosperity created surplus wealth that the beneficiaries of this growing affluence sought to use for their advantage. Therefore, the towns also became places where a marketplace could serve as a focal point for this process of exchanging excess food, or other assets, for other commodities. The result of these changes was an economic shift toward a mercantile economy, grounded upon the process of buying and selling, that gradually supplanted the feudal system and, simultaneously, challenged this former value system and replaced it with increasingly attractive beliefs that reflected this emerging economic and social reality.

Liberalism, Liberal Democracy, and Modern Legal Development

The success of this growing population of merchants, artisans, traders, and other people who became independent of the feudal system transformed European civilization, especially during the period of the Renaissance, beginning in the fifteenth century. Economic survival and prosperity was no longer a feature of being part of a broader agrarian structure. Success increasingly became a matter of individual achievement within the marketplace. Therefore, a person was not necessarily constrained by a socio-economic rank, conferred through the accident of birth.

This mercantile sector began to achieve economic domination. Its members experienced increased wealth, social ascendancy, and political power. They resented the continuation of feudal norms and institutions that attempted to limit the expression of their emerging status, particularly through the persistence of aristocratic rank and privilege. Therefore, they eagerly provided the impetus for political changes that would promote and protect the source of their economic and social success. Centralized governments, which had been relatively ineffectual, became beneficiaries of this trend. The advantage was mutual. Centralized political systems could enhance economically uniform standards, provide stability and protection on a national scale, ensure consistent regulation, a national system of transportation, a certain medium of exchange, and could advance the broader interests of international trade and commerce. This rising class of merchants, artisans, and traders (who, because their general status was conceived, socially, as falling between the medieval nobility and peasantry, became known as the "middle" class) could provide the financial backing that made this centralized political system feasible and effective, especially for overcoming the traditional dependence upon the aristocracy for revenue, advice, and military support. Thus these economic changes resulted in a political transformation.

This process prompted the development of a new set of widely held beliefs and values that reflected, and promoted, this transformation. The most basic of these values was an abstract conceptualization of "property." This value referred not only to commodities that people could physically own, but to anything a person could exchange for any other sort of "property." Labor could be included under this category, for, although it could not be measured or observed with any sort of empirical accuracy, it could be exchanged, nonetheless, for a wage. Intellectual efforts, likewise, could be exchanged, though they remained physically intangible. The centrality of "property" became the basis for all other considerations, since it was the key to the success of the mercantile economy. Therefore, its recognition and protection became a fundamental basis for supporting, and primary responsibility of, government.

"Property" would be a worthless concept if could not be readily exchanged. Feudal constraints, including the belief that everything ultimately belonged to feudal overlords, needed to be eliminated. This practical requirement of the marketplace was extended to the expectations persons began to hold concerning all aspects of their lives and existence as a community. Therefore, a demand for freedom from constraint became included among these prevailing values, and liberty became a core principle of this emerging ideological system.

The feudal system envisioned a stratified social and political structure, paralleling an equally stratified universe, in which personal identity was subsumed to the interest of accepting one's place as a component within the larger scheme. But the marketplace was perceived as functioning according to a different sort of interaction. Economic decisions are made, within this marketplace, upon an isolated basis. These interactions do not conform to a stable, machine-like order but are dependent upon a variety of influences and inclinations. The actions of the marketplace are not based upon predetermined status or rank, so they are not collectively driven. All people participating within it are evaluated upon the basis of their own merits and addressed according to the particulars of their own, unique situation. This emerging ideological system, therefore, needed to embrace a concept of individualism as an essential premise for political and social, as well as economic, purposes.

This liberty to dispense with one's own property on an individual basis would be useless, however, without the means to make *meaningful* decisions. The ability to exert control over oneself and the options available concerning any economic, political, or social situation is critical to the success of the marketplace and the society that springs from it. The negative emphasis of the value of liberty is balanced, therefore, by the positive emphasis of autonomy, which imposes certain obligations upon society and its government to maintain the means to operate effectively throughout this environment. Autonomy becomes, therefore, another defining value of this emerging ideological system.

Another fundamental value emerges as a consequence of the acceptance of these four key principles of "property," liberty, individualism, and autonomy. Success and failure within the marketplace ideally are determined by merit. Automatic advantages of rank or predetermined status may persist, but they are inconsistent with the premises of this ideological system and tend to be derided by the people who embrace it. Therefore, barriers to success that are externally imposed increasingly are rejected, especially when these obstacles result from apparently superficial characteristics, such as social status or racial identity. The value of equality becomes a difficult one to define, since it can be interpreted in terms of opportunity, as well as result. However, a general acceptance of some ideal of equality becomes a reasonably anticipated outcome of the other values and beliefs that comprise the core of this ideological heritage.

This accumulation of beliefs, values, and principles eventually would be articulated by philosophers and political theorists, especially by the seventeenth century, into a coherent ideology that derives its name from that core principle of liberty, so it became known as "liberalism"—literally, the ideology of freedom. While liberal democracy is a consequence of the evolution of a liberal society, it is not an automatic result. Provided that a government is constrained by liberal ideological values, its benefits theoretically should be enjoyed by all members of society. The notion that the very choice of a government and its policies should be determined by the sum of those persons who constitute the political society is a later development that occurred relatively gradually, and against a fair amount of resistance.

The explanation of liberalism through the allegorical device of the "social contract" became a means for making a connection (though, often, indirectly) with demands for democratic participation. Political theorists such as John Locke and Jean-Jacques Rousseau offered different ways to express this abstract construct, but the essential principle of a society and its government resulting from some form of consensus has remained a constant theme among them. The idea that a government is a creation of the people who comprise a society and the associated concept of governments exercising power through the consent of the government suggests, by itself, the logical extension of popular control that is the central premise of modern democracy. However, one obstacle to the full implementation of this principle is the capacity for defining and identifying those humans who are recognized as "persons," or full members of society whose rights are recognized and are able to participate in this democratic process.

These "persons" are defined in relation to the central liberal principle of "property." However, this definition is applied not just in terms of the fact that someone *possesses* property, but in terms of their recognized capacity to *bear* that property. People such as women, children, or slaves have, at various times, been acknowledged as having property, but have not been free to exchange that property. The extent of the electoral franchise (the members of society who may participate in the process of choosing a government) historically has been determined upon this basis.

More specifically, aside from the other disqualified groups (which include children, whose contracts must be enacted by adults representing their interests), the list of voters was determined, within most Western countries, upon the basis of the *amount* of property that could be demonstrably attached to a particular person. A certain amount of property was determined to be sufficient for establishing that a particular member of society had a large enough stake in the performance of government and its policies to warrant a role in shaping a system of government and selecting its officials. During the eighteenth century, for example, Great Britain limited the population eligible to vote for parliamentary representatives to relatively wealthy people. This level of the franchise was lowered as demands for democratic reform increased throughout British society, especially in 1831, 1867, and 1883, until any need for a property qualification for voting purposes was eliminated for all adult males, with women having their right to vote recognized by the early twentieth century.

Utilitarian ideas of the eighteenth and nineteenth centuries also promoted the continued development and acceptance of democratic principles. The empirical requirement for establishing "the greatest good for the greatest number" necessitated some sort of proof, and the need to seek an electoral "mandate" through of regular elections involving all members of society eventually became accepted as the most appropriate measurement of social good. Furthermore, as the surest means for protecting and promoting the fundamental principles of a liberal society, democracy presented the ideal which seemed, within that ideological context, to be truly "self-evident."

Law became the most important means for transmitting the evolving ideology of liberal democracy. The fact that law served as the means for indicating the distinction between public and private realms of society is, arguably, the most conspicuous example of this role. The fact that so much of the law is dedicated to the protection and regulation of "property" (even in its abstract sense) and the marketplace (especially in terms of contract law) is a profound testament to this relationship. The evolution of constitutional government was an even more prominent example, with constitutions, themselves, serving as the guarantors that the laws of a society would, indeed, conform to the expectations of a liberal democratic society.

Liberal democracy has become the most dominant ideological tradition in the world, especially by the twenty-first century. It has made strong inroads among non-Western communities, as well. Its core principles are relatively rudimentary, so a fair amount of variation among different expressions of liberal democratic thought are possible. These varying interpretations of this malleable ideological tradition include libertarian, republican, and communitarian variants that will not be addressed within other chapters of this book, especially the chapter devoted to rights and liberties. Meanwhile, it is important to grasp an understanding of this ideology at its most essential level. The fact that it is so dominant does not mean, however, that it is unchallenged. Other, constitutionally significant ideological traditions exist to compete with it, throughout the world. Therefore, a brief evaluation of the most important of these ideologies needs to be entertained.

Marxism and Law

Arguably, the most conspicuous ideological challenge to the dominance of liberal democracy has been Marxism. It was created in the nineteenth century, although many of its ideas are derived from beliefs and practices that long preceded its formal promulgation by Karl Marx. Its teachings are antithetical to the assumptions of liberal individualism, particularly regarding assumptions concerning "property" and its autonomous possession and use. It offered a revolutionary alternative that has inspired portentous political movements, especially during the twentieth century and particularly among developing countries. Its legal influence continues to be considerable, even following the late-twentieth-century demise of the Soviet Union.

Economic and political turmoil seemed to get steadily worse from the late-eighteenth through the mid-nineteenth centuries, especially throughout Europe, inspired both political unrest and intellectual response. One of these responses was articulated by Karl Marx, a German scholar who had emigrated to Great Britain to continue his agitation in support of the rights of workers and the replacement of the prevailing economic order. He offered an alternative interpretation of economic history as a prelude to this endeavor.

Marx had been a student of Georg Wilhelm Friedrich Hegel, the eminent German philosopher. Hegel argued that all, supposedly competing, philosophical systems actually represent phases of a philosophical development leading toward a comprehensive identification of *geist*, which translates roughly as an indication of human "spirit." This philosophical evolution has occurred, according to Hegel, as the result of dominant ideas, which he labeled as the "thesis," that generate an alternative response to the prevailing idea, labeled the "antithesis." This opposition eventually results in a merging of the two ideas, called the "synthesis," and the appearance of a new thesis, which prompts the response of an antithesis, perpetuates this historical cycle. The ultimate result should be, according to Hegel, a final amalgamation of all variations upon this human spirit, culminating in a "world *geist*" of shared beliefs, values, and a common human perspective.

Marx diverged from his former professor by insisting that economic activity was the determining feature of human history. He adapted Hegel's method, called the "dialectic," to his own study of economic history. The result was Marx's theory of "dialectical materialism," in which he determined that all human history is the saga of economic dominance and exploitation. The segment that controls the source of economic wealth also imposes a value system that rationalizes this dominance and the principles that bolster it. However, an alternative economic process becomes offered as an alternative, especially from that segment that does not enjoy the dominance of the current source of economic control.

The conflict between these economic alternatives results in the emergence of a new economic order, dominated, again, by a segment that finds itself, again, struggling to maintain that dominance against a rising alternative. The medieval European nobility, for example, controlled the land (thesis), which was the source of all economic activity. A small, but gradually growing, segment of the peasantry began to offer an alternative source of prosperity (antithesis) through the production and sale of commodities. The conflict for economic and political dominance resulted in the emergence of a mercantile economy of merchants, artisans, and traders which also included landowners and agricultural producers (synthesis), who now treated their land as yet another commodity, rather than the ultimate source of economic control. This segment of prominent "property" owners became the new thesis of this dialectical model, and the cycle continued.

The current "thesis" is, according to Marx, rooted in the control of capital and industrial capacity. Capitalism, as an economic system, rests upon a small class of investors and industrialists (whom Marx labelled the *bourgeoisie*) whose dominance is so complete that the rest of the population of workers (whom Marx labelled the *proletariat*) has no choice but to accept the wages and other terms they are offered, despite the illusion of control over their property, in the form of labor. These workers further have their "property" stolen from them, since their wages do not truly represent the value that has been generated from the industrial goods that are produced and sold. Capitalists and industrialists need to "steal" this labor-property, since it is the basis of their profits.

However, the ongoing need to maintain profits creates a tendency to diminish the wages of workers, further, thus depleting the marketplace of its own source of income, gradually undermining all economic activity, especially as the absence of ready capital increasingly is replaced with borrowed money, creating an overall economy resting upon an illusory foundation of credit. The illogic of this arrangement eventually will result in a collapse of the system and a subsequent elimination of all of the political institutions and cultural norms that support it, especially as the result of a violent revolution of the workers. The historic cycle is ended, replaced by a system in which individual ownership is abolished in favor of collective control of economic and political life.

Marx argued (often with the collaboration of Frederick Engels) that the dominance of the current capitalist system, its continued ability to exploit this "surplus value of labor," and the perpetuation of its control over the means of production depends upon the perpetuation of certain key deceptions. These "deceptions" stem from liberal democratic ideology, which serves as a prop for this economic order in the same way that government exists primarily for the purpose of maintaining the order and stability necessary for its perpetuation. These beliefs and values are, for Marx, examples of "false consciousness," including the misperception of individual identity, the concept of autonomous control of property, the true relevance and effectiveness of democratic control, the significance of non-economic sources of identity (including nationality, ethnicity, religion, and other features), and a trust in social and economic mobility.

Rather than perceiving themselves as autonomous individual persons, workers should come to recognize their collective character as part of a fundamental economic class, determined by their relationship to the means of production. This "class consciousness" is best fomented though the efforts of intellectual leaders, organizing a party for promoting these efforts, who will lead the workers (who have been kept in deliberate ignorance and incapacity) by assuming control of the means of production, following the overthrow of capitalism, resulting in the temporary presence of a "socialist" system and government controlled by the party for the benefit of the workers. This articulation of this phase of Marxist ideological development was refined by later theorists and activists, especially Lenin. The political and economic expediency of a socialist system will continue until the workers are ready to assume direct control of their collective economic destiny, without the need for government of any kind. This utopian vision of a "communist" society became the supreme goal of Marxist ideology.

The legal implications of this ideological system were profound. Since government is an instrument of economic will, its proper use should be to serve as a transitional support for the *proletariat*. As the population gains the ability to assume direct control over various facets of their economic, political, and social existence, the state will "wither away" by divesting itself of responsibility and eliminating the redundant institutions of government. Until that total condition has been reached, though, the government must continue to administer control of the means of production and of other legal and political activities, including the administration of justice.

The Marxist concept of justice is based upon the assumption that liberal legal norms are designed primarily to protect exclusive property interests, generally defining crime as a threat to those interests and assessing punishment as both protection of those interests and a means of compensation for lost property. Disputes will continue to exist among people, but the root of antagonism must be eliminated. Courts will lead parties to a dispute to arrive at a resolution that is fair for all parties, including the community, as a whole. The capitalist concept of private property is eliminated, but the contingency for people to possess certain goods, based upon their immediate needs, is accepted and mediated. Goods and services are derived from all members of society according to their specific talents and ability to provide it; they are distributed according to each person's needs, rather than specific capacities. The judicial system makes certain that this principle is upheld, especially in the mediation of disputes.

The legal system must protect the whole community, and not just a dominant economic class. Persons whose activities seek to undermine the advance toward the elimination of private ownership (by hoarding wealth, stealing from society or other people, and sabotaging collective economic policies) must be prevented from performing this harmful activity. Violent acts also must be stopped and, if necessary, punished. But crimes are committed against the entire community, rather than against specific persons; since the state transitionally acts on behalf of the people, legal violations inevitably are interpreted as assaults upon the government and the entire working class that it serves. In practice, much of the activity of the legal and judicial systems of a socialist system, under the influence of Marxist ideology, resembles many of the conventional features of liberal democratic legal and judicial institutions. But the ultimate purpose is defined very differently, so the actual implementation of socialist legal and judicial activities diverges from them, especially in terms of legal interpretation and the focus upon its final effect concerning overall economic policies and goals.

A Marxist legal tradition seeks to counter the perceived trend of economic exploitation through the manipulation of private property. It shapes a society that presumably is preparing for the eventual elimination of formal government. It is grounded upon ideological beliefs and values that emphasize class consciousness, collective economic control, and freedom derived from the elimination of exploitation and the predetermined life choices that result from it. This ideal, however, arguably has not been translated fully into attempts at creating socialist countries and the constitutions that supposedly give them legal expression.

The Soviet Union may have collapsed, for example, because of its own exploitation of the people, in contradiction of true Marxist principles, although liberal democratic countries often are accused of similar perversions of the principles that they constitutionally extol. Nonetheless, the influence of Marxist ideology should not be underestimated, even following the demise of the Soviet Union, for it continues to dominate certain significant legal systems and it still offers, arguably, the most effective ideological and legal alternative to the otherwise dominant liberal democratic tradition.

Classic Conservatism and Law

The terms "liberal" and "conservative" generally are misapplied and misunderstood in common parlance, especially as used by journalists and popular political commentators. This less accurate use of these terms does not refer to true ideological distinctions but to alternative interpretations and applications from within a particular ideological tradition, especially liberal democracy. Nonetheless, an ideologically meaningful conservative tradition does exist, and it can be termed as a "classic" expression as a means of distinguishing it from more pedestrian references.

Conservative thought emerged within Europe, during the sixteenth and seventeenth centuries, in response to the decline of feudal ideals and institutions and reaction against the growing popularity of liberal principles and practices.

Proponents of this ideological tradition did not seek to retain the rigid structures and values of the medieval period but to ameliorate the perceived inadequacies and dangers inherent in a rapid transition toward a less constrained society. Conservatives were not diametrically opposed to liberal values but were deeply concerned about the consequences of an uncritical and unrestrained imposition of them that could lead to a society lacking control, order, stability, security, and those general conditions conducive to peace and prosperity. Political theorists such as Thomas Hobbes alleged that the chaos surrounding the breakdown of authority during the English Civil War revealed the need for a dominant sovereign to prevent people from becoming victims of their own immoderate and self-destructive tendencies.

Conservatives conceive of the relationship between a sovereign and its subjects in much the same way as the relationship between a father and his children. A good father imposes limits upon his children and their behavior for their own protection and welfare. However, in order to allow them to grow and mature, he also grants them a measure of freedom. These children, within the constraints ordained by paternal care, are free to conduct their lives as they wish, including a right to experiment in personal conduct, engage in relationships, protect and promote their own interests, and make other sorts of personal choices. In fact, their very ability to enjoy these benefits and this freedom depends upon the stable environment that the father provides. Therefore, they owe their father unquestioned obedience, even when they believe (usually incorrectly) that paternal actions are unwarranted, unfair, or contrary to their own immediate interests. Otherwise, their lack of judgment and maturity would lead them to make decisions and engage in conduct that could prove to be harmful to themselves and others, resulting in a chaotic environment in which true growth, development, and safety are impossible.

Classic conservatives emphasize this need for restraint, especially in terms of "prudent" responses toward threats and opportunities. A father often employs the supportive tools of religion, the extended family structure, familial traditions and loyalties, and other means of reinforcing this sense of restraint. Likewise, traditional social, political, and, even, religious institutions serve the same purpose for the sovereign. Change is possible, even the change envisioned by liberal ideological beliefs and values (such as the role of the marketplace and the preeminent position of "property" and the concept of rights related to it), but within the structure that these traditional conventions, customs, and establishments provide. Therefore, the pace of change is moderated, so it may be sustained without threatening peace, stability, and order.

The discarding of those institutions that connect a people with their past, according to conservative theorists such as Edmund Burke, merely invites the exploitation of the weak and the lack of proper authority. Burke argued that this often traditionally sanctioned authority actually is necessary for achieving the goals of those people who seek change. However, such change must be made within existing institution and subject to the unchallenged discretion of the sovereign. Otherwise, given the brutal tendencies of human nature, the result can be a disastrous loss of stability and security, as Burke noted in relation to the disorder and destruction that accompanied the Reign of Terror, during the French Revolution, and its attendant elimination of the traditional institutions of French society, including the monarchy, the political role of the Gallican Church, and the supposedly stabilizing influence of the former governmental system.

Only the sovereign should be free from constraint, and a classic conservative concept of the "social contract" emphasizes this complete submission of a people to government authority. The nature of this sovereign authority can be varied (it even can be democratic in nature), but its power must remain unchallenged and unquestioned. A successful sovereign will be generous, rather than tyrannical—otherwise, the sovereign ultimately will rule a society that is unable, through its dilapidation, or unwilling, through its lack of an incentive to loyalty, to lend support to it in times of crisis. Individual identity expression is permitted, but it is tempered through a broader collective identity with the various significant segments and groups that constitute the society. This identity can be based upon economic status, geographical loyalties, social status (including traditional aristocratic and commoner rankings), and other collective perspectives. Nonetheless, a successful government recognizes all of these groups and attempts to be inclusive in response to them.

The legal effect of conservative ideology focuses upon the emphasis of sovereign authority. A constitution, for example, should not limit the government; instead, it should reinforce its dominant role to provide support for its responsibilities, as well as identifying that role for the benefit of all subject groups and people. The judicial system serves a critical role of enforcing necessary stability and security, especially against people who would challenge the interests of society, as protected and promoted by the sovereign. This legal heritage remains particularly strong among Latin American countries, especially as reinforced by a traditional interpretation of Roman Catholic theological norms. Individual rights and privileges may be invoked and upheld, but the sovereign, and not individual people, has the final authority regarding interpreting and, even, permitting them. Crimes are not regarded as having been committed against other people as much as they are treated as attacks upon the general peace and prosperity of the community.

Opposition to the sovereign in ways that are not constitutionally mandated, in particular, are fiercely enjoined, and treason becomes a common charge against even peaceful resistance to traditional institutions of state and society. Yet conservative ideology is cited by its proponents as an actual guarantor of human freedom, by providing the peace, stability, and prosperity necessary for all people to achieve their desires. It also accommodates good relations among all members of society, including among segments and groups that might, otherwise, find themselves in mutually destructive conflict. The legal and judicial systems, supported by the police power of the sovereign, ensures that condition through the enforcement of laws that are influenced by these conservative beliefs and values, and the constitutional system provides its ultimate definition and impetus.

Feminism and Law

The ideological challenge of gender has not resulted in any specific legal system or, even, offered an alternative to the prevailing legal traditions. This ideological approach is based upon the perception that gender, in fact, matters, not only in terms of advancing a more complete and inclusive grasp of the human condition but, also, in terms of reevaluating other ideological assumptions. Therefore, the constitutional significance of feminist thought depends upon the receptiveness of the ideological foundations of different legal traditions to the claims and challenges that gender provides, especially in terms of advancing the dignity and interests of women against the trend of male dominance and gender inequality.

The feminist challenge to liberal democracy has been one of the most prominent approaches of this challenge. The first task of the earliest advocates of a feminist perspective, especially during the eighteenth and nineteenth centuries, addressed the status of women, and not just men, as "property bearers." This consideration helped to increase the relevance of liberal debates concerning the significance and meaning of "equality" as an ideological and, consequently, legal and political principle. This challenge does not seek to displace liberal democratic ideological norms but, instead, confronts liberal democratic societies with the premise of making these societies and their values inclusive of all persons, both female and male.

A different sort of feminist approach gained prominence during the twentieth century. These feminist theorists rejected all conventional ideologies, including liberal democracy, as being inescapably male dominated, particularly since the premises of their value systems were constructed by men, from a male perspective, and for the exclusive benefit of men. They have argued that the perceptual and experiential centrality of gender requires a complete departure from the explanations and justifications of these established ideological systems in favor of beliefs and values that are truly reflective of a uniquely female perception. Because these feminist theorists advocate a conceptual departure from customary ideological assumptions in favor of the advancement of feminism *as* an ideological (for lack of a better term) approach, itself, they often are identified as "radical" feminists who have broken entirely with conventional methods of established philosophical analysis.

Both liberal feminists and radical feminists contend that legal systems generally offer male patterns of interpretation as being "neutral" or, even, "normal." Characteristics of this male legal perspective include a tendency to express legal concepts in abstract terms, requiring a conformity of circumstances to rules that must be applicable in all circumstances. A female perspective arguably is more contextual, allowing for variances in circumstance, environment, and relationship—replacing sterile, abstruse, male-oriented doctrines of evaluating a legal controversy with the dictum of "it depends."

Another male characteristic of legal interpretation is the tendency to rank ethical concerns according to a hierarchy of meaning and preference, rather than contextualizing ethical issues, particularly in terms of outcomes and the effect of these choices upon people, their needs, and their relationships. The rule-based approach to law is indicative of the underlying premises of legal positivism, which seeks to remove legal matters from the "corrupting" influences of intuitive and emotional considerations. Many feminist legal scholars seek to temper that sterile method, with its competitive overtones, in favor of a more cooperative understanding of law as a tool for mediation and reconciliation of disputes and difficulties.

One of the most troubling abstractions detected from a liberal legal perspective is a concept described as the "sexual contract." By treating marriage as a contractual arrangement between two people, human relationships and sexuality are reduced to "property" that can be exchanged as commodities. This legal interpretation of marriage predates the rise of liberal ideology, but the notion that a woman's sexuality (as suggested by the term "marital duty" as a euphemism for sexual intercourse within marriage) is exchanged for a man's obligation to provide for, and protect, her (as represented by the concept of a dowry and the ceremonial "giving away" of a bride from a father to a husband) has been bolstered by the more abstract expectations of proprietary interests advanced under liberalism.

The broad legal implications of these critiques, especially for defining the role of women within a society, are considerable. Ongoing debates about the meaning of equality, especially when the category of gender is included, reveal the significance of this ideological challenge. Both liberal feminist and radical feminist responses offer important challenges to prevailing ideological foundations of the legal systems of modern countries.

Assessing Ideological Evaluations of Law

Other ideological traditions also could be included within this appraisal, including anarchism, which challenges the very idea of law and any need for such coercive institutions. Furthermore, non-Western philosophical influences have been addressed within the chapter on Eastern legal traditions and will be examined within the chapters on tribal law and Western religion and law. The philosophical expressions of law often cannot be reduced merely to the declaration of an easily identified set of ideological principles. However, a facile dismissal of this relationship would be equally superficial.

A myriad of sources of legal beliefs, values, and principles must be undertaken for the purpose of useful comparative legal analysis, from throughout the world. But Western ideologies, initially emerging from the modern European experience, are especially notable, because of their influence upon legal systems throughout the rest of the world. Whether this inclination is a pernicious example of Western cultural and legal imperialism or merely a result of a global desire to choose from among attractive alternatives, the effusion of this relationship between law and ideology should not be ignored. Otherwise, a truly meaningful comparison of modern legal traditions, including non-Western ones, will be, arguable, impractical or, even, futile.

References

Andrew Altman, *Critical Legal Studies: A Liberal Critique*. Princeton, NJ, Princeton University Press, 1990.
Daniel J. Boorstin, *The Mysterious Science of the Law: An Essay on Blackstone's Commentaries*. Chicago, University of Chicago Press, 1996.
Hugh Collins, *Marxism and Law*. Oxford, Oxford University Press, 1984.
Martin van Hees, *Rights and Decisions: Formal Models of Law and Liberalism*. Dordrecht, The Netherlands, Kluwer Academic, 1995.
Paul Q. Hirst, *On Law and Ideology*. Atlantic Highlands, NJ, Humanities Press, 1979.
Martin Loughlin, *Public Law and Political Theory*. Oxford, Clarendon Press, 1992.
Catharine A. MacKinnon, *Toward a Feminist Theory of the State*. Cambridge, MA, Harvard University Press, 1989.
C. B. Macpherson, *The Life and Times of Liberal Democracy*. Oxford, Oxford University Press, 1989.
Susan Marks, *The Riddle of All Constitutions: International Law, Democracy, and the Critique of Ideology*. Oxford, Oxford University Press, 2000.
Susan Millns and Noel Whitty, eds., *Feminist Perspectives on Public Law*. London, Cavendish, 1999.
Evgenii Bronislavovich Pashukanis, *Law and Marxism: A General Theory*, Barbara Einhorn, trans., Chris Arthur, ed. London, Pluto, 1989.
Thomas W. Simon, *Law and Philosophy: An Introduction with Readings*. New York, McGraw-Hill, 2001.
Mark Tebbit, *Philosophy of Law: An Introduction*. New York, Routledge, 2000.

CHAPTER 5

Common Law Systems

Competing Structural Expressions of Law

The two most prevalent institutional expressions of law throughout the modern world are the common law and civil law systems. Generally, texts on comparative law focus the preponderance of their coverage to a structural analysis of these two systems. However, from the vantage of a broader exploration of law (especially public law), the need to devote that much contemplation is diminished. Nonetheless, a meaningful analysis of these contrasting institutional approaches to the practical workings of the law cannot be ignored, nor should the significance of this subject be underestimated. The choice of one system over the other offers a very relevant insight into the overall nature of a legal system, giving its ideals and directives practical application, expression, and context.

Legal practitioners often are most interested in this level of comparison, for it has the most practical application to their professional concerns. The most notable difference between major legal systems seems to involve their institutional structures and legal rules. However, other significant differences also must be considered. Historical circumstances responsible for a system, especially in terms of political and cultural goals, are decisive. The structure and operation of the institutions that apply and interpret the law should be evaluated, specifically, especially in terms of the assumptions about law and human nature that can be derived from them. The type of legal education necessary to function as a practitioner within the legal system also is an important indicator. The ultimate source of the legal principles and ideas often poses the most telling feature of the legal system, especially since it is the genesis of all other legal thought and interpretation.

These features establish the broad categories for identifying the two most dominant forms of legal systems. Other variations are possible, but the common law and civil law, broadly defined, are the systems that have prevailed throughout the world. Each structure is shaped to serve its respective political and legal traditions, while the constitutional systems produced by these political traditions also are affected by the basic legal system that usually has preceded their formal development. Either system could be evaluated first, but the preponderance of popular images of the American courtroom, especially through novels, films, and television, suggest that the common law system may be a more generally familiar one, even within some civil law countries. Therefore, it may be easier to start with an examination of this arguably more popularly represented legal system, its antecedents, and its assumptions.

Historical Development of the Common Law System

England is the home of the common law system. England developed a sense of national identity earlier than most of continental Europe, yet, by the twelfth century, it still lacked true political unity, despite the military success of the Norman invaders who had gained control during the previous century. King Henry II was determined to promote a unified political structure, and his plan included a centralization of the law.

English law, prior to the twelfth century, was an amalgamation of local and regional customs, consistent with the tribal heritage of the various peoples who had settled this land. Henry and his judicial officials were content to allow these local legal norms to prevail, provided they could be subject to an ultimate central jurisdiction. Henry established tribunals that would have supreme jurisdiction over all legal disputes. However, he wanted to ensure that his subjects would accept this jurisdiction willingly, so he established this authority upon the basis of the general legal principles and rules that these various regions and communities already established.

This unified legal and judicial system needed to reconcile these variations. Rather than imposing an alien body of law upon the entire country, Henry left this process to the discretion of his judicial officers. They would consider, particularly, appeals of the decisions of local judicial authorities and attempt to reconcile them with the rules and principles of other jurisdictions. The simplest means for achieving this goal was to discover those aspects of legal ideals and reasoning that these jurisdictions appeared to share, using those shared principles, derived from historical practice and the settlement of previous legal disputes, as a basis for establishing a unified ruling that could be applicable to all English communities that fell under this centralized jurisdiction.

These jurists traveled throughout the realm, within their own "circuits" of appellate jurisdiction, establishing this body of shared legal rules and principles and imposing them upon all of the specific legal controversies they considered. These royal magistrates were careful to keep their own rulings consistent with legal opinions that had been established, previously, and used these prior decisions as a basis for these overriding, unifying legal standards. This recourse to previous judicial rulings became the foundation for this system of law and jurisprudence, signified by the Latin expression *stare decisis*, roughly meaning "let the decision stand." This reliance upon previous judicial rulings, or "precedence," became a defining feature of this legal and judicial system that sought to base the law upon a set of rules and principles that all English communities already, in one or another form, shared—in other words, it was based upon a "common" law.

Certain centralized judicial institutions were established in support of this legal development. They served a dual purpose of increasing royal authority over the entire country while, also, reinforcing these "common" legal principles within specialized areas. The Exchequer Court adjudicated disputes arising from revenues and the Court of Common Pleas assumed responsibility for title disputes, while the King's Bench passed final judgment upon other public legal controversies. These three courts were not consistently used, nor did they tend to interfere with the feudal privileges often exercised through local judicial organs. But, as extensions of the theoretically overriding authority of the *Curia Regis*, or "King's Court" (which tended to be confined to matters directly affecting the security of the throne and realm), they reaffirmed the central authority of the sovereign while instilling a rudimentary sense of national unity through this process. The legal rulings of the king's judicial representatives assumed a final authority that overrode contrary decisions of lower judicial officials, and these unifying opinions served as precedents for later monarchs and their judiciary to apply toward subsequent legal contests.

The "writ system" bolstered this centralizing claim. Subjects seeking the king's justice could make a formal request for a writ to be issued by appropriate royal officials, deriving their prerogative from the monarch's most senior judicial minister, the Lord High Chancellor. This process was intended to transfer the setting for addressing a legal dispute to the domain of this royal system of courts. It also established consistent procedures (originally cited as "forms of action") and the formulation of the principle that a particular process was "due" to each petitioner benefiting from the command of the writ. A body of rules emerged, promoting a system that could be recognizable, certain, and relatively fair. At first, the issuance of writs was based solely upon privilege; gradually, it became the basis for commanding the application of common legal procedures regarding all matters of law and justice.

The growing power of Parliament, throughout the medieval and modern periods, also grounded the common law in statutes and other legislative guidance. However, while legislation indicated policy, common law precedents continued to provide the legal rules and judicial principles that allowed judges to interpret and apply this legislation to actual controversies that came before their courts. The political purposes of the evolution of this legal system were clarified, both in terms of strengthening ongoing aspirations of national unity but also providing a sense of political continuity for English subjects, even as the historic struggle for the ultimate expression of sovereign authority between executive and legislative forces intensified.

Another important legal development emerged to complement or oppose (depending upon one's perspective) the growth of the common law and its judicial system. Participants in a dispute who were displeased with the outcome of a legal ruling of a lower court had recourse to petition the monarch through the Lord High Chancellor. These appeals were made to the legal office of that august office of the Chancery, generally based upon the claim that a technically correct legal decision might, nonetheless, be grossly unfair, according to broader, non-legal criteria of justice and morality. The Chancery grew increasingly accustomed, especially during the later medieval period, to making "corrections" of decisions emerging from the common law system by developing a parallel doctrine that determined the precise nature of remedies, penalties, and, occasionally, substantive legal outcomes upon the basis of a sense of fair, or "equal," results.

This emphasis upon "equitable" standards resulted in the emergence of the jurisdiction of Courts of Equity, deriving their authority directly from royal prerogative. This process was conceived as a corrective to legal rulings that appeared to offend other, widely accepted standards of probity and a broader concept of "natural justice" that seemed to emanate (though, often, vaguely) from the theoretical natural law tradition. But the actual decisions generally relied upon the inclination of the individual adjudicator, so this standard of equity became increasingly regarded as being inconsistent and, even, arbitrary.

However, the perceived need to reconcile strict legal rules and precedents with culturally and politically acceptable standards of fairness, as well as a desire to compromise the underlying political competition between the legislatively favored common law system with the executively favored role of Chancery, led to the adoption of standards of equity into the institutionally established judicial system, particularly as an increasingly systematized standard, with its own emerging principle of precedent, that could aid judges in their task of interpreting legislation and common law principles.

By the nineteenth century, the common law system achieved an institutional presence that, through ongoing reforms of the judiciary (including the final merging of the Chancery with the courts), reached its current standard of stability, consistency, and popular legitimacy. Furthermore, the expansion of the British Empire and other extensions of British influence spread the essential features of this legal system to other prominent countries, including the United States. These features, both institutional and theoretical, are most visibly present through the general activities of the court systems.

Structure and Practices of the Judicial System

Common law system courts can be divided into two broad categories of jurisdiction: original and appellate. Courts of original jurisdiction are trial courts. They consider matters of both "fact" and "law." This distinction is important. Matters of "fact" are actions, incidents, circumstances, motives, or any other human activity associated with a legal dispute. They can include deeds involved in the alleged committing of a crime, or behavior producing injury or damage, or features like time, place, physical conditions, or even descriptions of emotions, professional opinions, medical evaluations, or other empirically demonstrable or personally asserted considerations that can be evaluated by other people. "Facts" thus constitute the legal concept of "evidence" that lie at the core of a trial.

"Law," however, refers to the legal source and context of the dispute. It can include judicial procedure (including "rules of evidence" establishing parameters and guidelines for evaluation of evidence), legislation or statutes that define the actual crime or civil offense under dispute, jurisprudential interpretations of the relevant legislation or statute, other relevant legal (including constitutional) principles and limits (including rights and liberties), and provisions for the overall control of the trial process. Courts of original jurisdiction, or trial courts, feature both of these elements in their legal determinations.

Courts of appellate jurisdiction generally consider only matters of "law" and will address matters of "fact" solely (with certain rare exceptions) to provide an empirical context for evaluating the "law." They will consider, for example, whether or not certain evidence should have been evaluated, at all, during a trial, given legal principles that govern the types of evidence that are permitted to be presented or the circumstances that make attaining and presenting that evidence valid. Appellate courts can overturn the conclusions reached by trial courts on the basis of serious errors they detect regarding matters of law. This action can result in ordering a new trial, amending a directed remedy, or the complete invalidation of the conclusion determined by the trial court. Appellate courts can overrule courts of original jurisdiction, but only within the parameters appropriate to their role and limited to the evaluation of legal practices and principles.

The jurisdiction of courts within a common law system are, largely, geographically determined. Courts of original jurisdiction tend to be most numerous and, therefore, each one serves a relatively small physical area, although some appellate courts also can serve as trial courts in certain areas as prescribed under the prevailing constitutional order. Often, these areas of jurisdiction conform to some other political boundary, such as a county, province, state, municipality, or some other division.

Although some specialized courts do exist within common law systems (especially at the level of original jurisdiction and in certain areas of administrative law, economic policy, and the military), the norm is for all courts within the system to be responsible for adjudicating all areas of law and all legal disputes that arise within the geographical area that constitutes the jurisdictions of these courts, both criminal and civil. Generally, the larger area of responsibility (resulting from the grouping of a certain number of smaller jurisdictions of trial courts) will be placed under the appellate jurisdiction of a higher-level court.

Thus a single court exercises appellate responsibility over several trial courts, all within a broadly defined geographical area. Finally, a common law system places, over all of these appellate courts and their broader geographical jurisdictions, a single court of final appeal, with a jurisdiction that encompasses the entire judicial and political system. The number of the levels of all of these courts may vary, but they are united under this concept of a highest court that reconciles differences among the interpretations that emanate from these lower courts. This unity of interpretive jurisdiction is an essential feature of a common law system. The conformity of legal principles that is imposed, ultimately, in this way is bolstered by the character of the process that trains and guides legal practitioners for a career as common law jurists.

Legal Education and Training

Traditionally, common law systems have emphasized "experience" over formal education as the primary method for preparing legal practitioners. Lawyers were produced from a process of apprenticeship, like the practitioners of many other skilled professions. English legal practitioners achieved their standing, eventually, through becoming attached to, and studying under, established lawyers at one of the four Inns of Court (where the category of lawyer known as barristers maintained their offices and aspiring legal practitioners were expected to reside and learn from supervised self-study and observation), as regulated by professional, rather than academic, authorities, including the Law Society, which regulates that category of lawyers known as solicitors.

Academic education has not been, historically, the path toward membership within the legal profession. Those persons aspiring to a legal career were tested, following their period of "apprenticeship," in order to be permitted to approach the "bar" of the court as one of its acknowledged officers. The "bar exam" remains the culmination of the process for becoming a legal practitioner within common law systems. Increasingly, though, legal practitioners generally have been required to have degrees in higher education, including, today, some form of specialized law degree.

However, a university degree in law does *not* qualify a person to practice law within a common law system. These persons still *must* be tested, separately, upon their *practical* knowledge of, and abilities within, the law—the same sort of knowledge that an apprentice is expected to attain. Presently, lawyers generally achieve their professional credentials through the combination of achieving a formal law degree, followed by professional evaluation in the form of a certification examination, though persons who become lawyers by "reading" the law and taking the bar exam without the benefit of a formal law degree persist in some places.

Therefore, the theme of "experience" over formal education for purposes of governing the profession and its practitioners remains dominant within the common law system. Advancement within the legal profession also is based upon this theme of professional experience. That theme is consistent with the central principle of *stare decisis* that guides the development of the common law, itself. An awareness of precedent and its cumulative character, as well as the most appropriate methods for applying it to the interpretation of law, would seem, according to conventional wisdom, best learned through habitual practice and routine, rather than explicit study and application of theoretical principles, as gained through a university.

The selection of judges and other senior jurists also is based upon their practical experience and proven competence, rather than any formal, institutional training or education. Even when judges are elected, rather than the conventional method of appointment (either by or, often, with the guidance and approval of the legal system's governing body of the legal profession) their preliminary eligibility for seeking office generally is based upon completion of a considerable number of years of service as lawyers. The prestige of judges, drawn from their experience, parallels the experience that serves as a base for all professional legal credentials within the common law system.

Legal Procedures and Structures

The formal process of the common law system, especially in terms of trials, is well known to many people, even from countries that have not adopted this system. Popular films that depict American trials and the activities of American lawyers have been particularly effective in conveying an impression of the methods and rules associated with this sort of jurisprudence. But its true distinctiveness can be lost from this artistic representation, so a better understanding should be articulated.

The common law judicial process is described as an "accusatorial" system. In practice, it resembles an athletic competition, with two opposing sides, each seeking to win under conditions that have been made as "even" as possible, following standard rules that apply to both sides, and contested under the guidance of a "referee" who is designated to enforce the rules in a fair and neutral fashion, ultimately resulting in a conclusion to this contest that produces a "winner" and a "loser." Some observers might object to this characterization, but popular perceptions of trials under this system and, even, the perceived attitudes and approaches of the professional participants, appear to support this analogy. The "contestants" include the prosecution and defense (in a criminal case) or the plaintiff and defendant (in a civil case), with the judge serving as "referee." However, the ultimate declaration of a "winner" is left to another body involved within this process—the jury.

Criminal proceedings begin with an arrest or indictment of an accused person, who, once taken into custody, must be charged and arraigned. This part of the procedure conforms to the principle of *habeas corpus*, first guaranteed within England by the Magna Carta of 1215. Arrested persons must be physically produced, informed of the charges made against them, and asked to declare (or "plead") their guilt or innocence. A timetable for the subsequent trial is publicly scheduled, unless the accused person pleads "guilty," in which case arrangements for determining a penalty are made. The formal trial begins after the prosecution (representing the sovereign authority of the state) and the defense have gathered and evaluated evidence, made their preparations, and, often, conferred with each other, especially for the potential purpose of reaching an agreement (such as a "plea bargain") that will avert the need for a trial.

During the trial, evidence is presented by both sides, including the calling of witnesses, in an attempt to confirm the charges or demonstrate a reasonable doubt of the validity of those charges. The context of presenting this evidence is determined by the legislation that describes the alleged crime, the rules of procedure established for trials and other, relevant legal principles that affect a particular legal controversy, including matters of civil guarantees, public policy, and rights and liberties. Two sources of authority operate as part of the trial. The judge, as already described, controls the overall proceedings as a neutral arbiter of the law. The jury, consisting of a body of legal lay persons, evaluates the evidence within the broader legal context that the judge provides.

Judges generally limit their evaluation to these matters of law. They uphold procedural rules, particularly when one side or the other challenges them or charges that the other side is violating these rules, usually with the familiar interjection of the word "objection!" These rules can include the types of evidence that can be introduced, the way in which evidence is presented (including the examination of witnesses), the propriety of certain aspects of trial strategy, and the effect of these procedures upon the interests of the public and the rights of accused persons.

Judges also maintain courtroom decorum, and they are responsible for "instructing" the jury, particularly in terms of directing them in their obligations and responsibilities and providing them with an explanation of the relevant statute that defines the crime that the defendant has been accused of violating. Judges also consider other procedural and substantive challenges, including requests to dismiss the charges for lack of evidence, ordering a new trial because of an inconclusive or tainted result (known as a "mistrial"), the desire of defendants to change their pleas, challenges to the interpretation and applicability of the relevant statutes, and other matters.

The jury becomes the evaluator of the "facts." Traditionally, the jury consists of persons who are the accused person's "peers," although this term has become somewhat anachronistic within modern democratic societies. During the period of this system's medieval origins, the members of the jury were supposed to share the same social status as the accused person (current members of the British nobility still may insist upon a jury consisting solely of other members of the nobility), but, within a post-feudal context, that concept has lost its meaning, although it also may be applied to the belief that members of a jury should include persons who share a socio-economic background with the defendant. Another tradition that developed was the concept of a jury consisting of twelve persons, although that number is subject to variation.

The members of the jury apply the evidence presented to them to the description of the crime and the other relevant legal principles that the judge has described to them. A criminal case usually requires that they apply a standard of "guilt beyond a reasonable doubt," while a civil case often substitutes a less stringent standard of a "preponderance of the evidence" for reaching a final determination. Juries generally, but not always, must reach a unanimous conclusion within a criminal case, though only a majority of them often are needed for making a final determination within a civil case. This determination of "guilt" or "innocence," or (in a civil case) a finding for the plaintiff or the defendant, results in a "verdict" (from the Latin word for "truth") which subsequently is reported to the judge and, then, to all other interested parties. Sometimes, juries also are asked to determine or recommend an appropriate penalty, if relevant, although that responsibility traditionally belongs to the judge, who can apply varying criteria and circumstances to the sentencing parameters established by penal statutes or precedent.

Civil cases resemble most of the features of a criminal case, but significant differences exist. The sovereign does not participate as an active competitor in the process, unless the sovereign is acting as a private interest. Defendants may not be incarcerated, since a crime is not involved, but they may be required to provide compensation in the form of an award or monetary penalties. Specific rules of procedure and evidence can differ, especially since the standards for determining a verdict are based upon the settling of a private dispute (although it could have public consequences), rather than the struggle between a defendant's liberty and the safety of society. Often, in a civil case, the judge serves the dual role of judge *and* jury, especially when all parties concur with that arrangement and the contested sum is relatively small.

Some minor (or "petty") criminal cases also may find the judge serving both as judge and jury, though, again, such as arrangement generally involves the concurrence of all parties, particularly the defendant. As already noted, the standard for determining a verdict within a civil case usually differs from a criminal case, with a plaintiff simply needing to reach a standard of establishing a preponderance of evidence, rather than the standard of guilt beyond a reasonable doubt that a prosecutor generally must establish. Furthermore, the jury need not be united in its final determination within a civil case, necessarily, and it often plays a more active role in determining the amount of a penalty or award, should the plaintiff prevail.

The decisions reached by a trial court may be appealed. Both criminal and civil cases may be brought before the same court, and the geographically determined appellate courts generally consider appeals from all categories of trials and hearings, including administrative law. Generally, an appellate court consists of a panel of judges, and a majority ruling is needed to reach a conclusion regarding an appeal. Juries do not exist at the appellate level, since appeal courts generally may not review challenges to evidence. Only issues of legal procedure, principles, and other matters of "law" may be considered. These matters may include constitutional requirements (such as rights and liberties), misinterpretation of precedent, a faulty admission of evidence (in which case the evidence, itself, may be indirectly considered), a violation of "due process," or other "errors" made during the trial phase, especially by the presiding judge.

The results of a criminal trial generally can be appealed only by the defense, although the prosecution can challenge the decisions of a trial judge or jury regarding the specific sentence. Either party can appeal the decision reached during a civil trial. Beyond the immediate appellate court exists at least one (occasionally more) higher level of appellate jurisdiction, and the decision of the appeal court can be further appealed to a court at that level. Appeals ultimately can be made to the highest court of appeal, which makes the definitive judicial determinations for all legal challenges, imposed upon the entire judicial system and all of its courts. Appeals courts are not required to consider appeals that arise (and usually are made as a matter of routine) from the decisions reached by a trial court, and they have a process for determining the actual cases they will accept for such consideration, especially if a profound question of law, constitutionality, or some other controversial and consequential legal issue is at stake.

Judges at both the trial and appellate levels are preoccupied with the interpretation of the law. This interpretation is based upon a variety of sources that challenge their experience and the knowledge and wisdom they gain from that experience. These sources both assist and constrain this process, and they are the most conspicuously important features of the common law system, so they need to be particularly appreciated.

Sources of Law

The core principle of *stare decisis*, or "precedent," previously has been described as a defining feature of the common law system. The written opinions of judges, especially at the appellate level, are permeated with references to judicial opinions from prior cases. These references provide the justification for rulings on legal concepts that have been addressed and, in fact, actually defined by other jurists, from the perspective of other legal controversies.

But judges citing precedent need to apply these previous opinions to the specific circumstances of the case they are considering at that moment. Therefore, they need to provide their own, personal interpretation, adaptation, and definition for these rules and ideas. Simply citing a prior case and the previous opinion of a jurist within it normally proves to be insufficient for the purpose of providing a true basis for the law. Opinions and rulings taken from sources other than actual judicial cases also may be employed as part of the process of *stare decisis*, but this fact still does not satisfy the need for interpretive guidelines, nor does it offer the additional sources of legal interpretation that are, obviously, still needed.

Different techniques have been developed as methods of judicial interpretation. One broad approach has been labeled "interpretivist." This method emphasizes the "original meaning" of the rules, principles, or, more often, statutes and legislation as they were originally conceived, and tries to remain as close as possible to that intent. This meaning can be derived from the drafters of legislation, the jurists who first formulated a legal concept, or the general socio-economic, political, and philosophical climate of the general community within which this concept was forged. Judges who prefer this method for evaluating precedent and legislation often argue that it prevents them from imposing personal preferences and biases upon this process of interpretation, so they avoid supplanting the will of the sovereign.

Another broad approach has been labeled "activist." It emphasizes the need to keep the law relevant by adapting it to alterations of the values and needs of an ever-changing society. These judges argue that the law should not be held captive by the past but remain the domain of an evolving tradition and a living people and their jurists. Variations of this method include such innovative techniques as "legal realism," which evaluates legislation and legal issues by their actual results, rather than their intent, òr "command." These judges take into account the social, political, economic, cultural, and philosophical implications of their opinions upon the people who actually will be affected by them. Both of these approaches often are far more relevant to the interpretation of constitutional precedents than to more basic concepts, principles, and rules of law. Nonetheless, these intellectual conditions play an important role in the overall process of "judge made" law that is highly indicative of the common law system. However, precedent, in any context, is not the sole source of legal ideas and principles within the common law system.

Statutes, legislation, and regulations actually can override precedent by imposing politically determined definitions of legal norms and principles. Regulations, in particular, are written by public administrators, with the approval of the sovereign, and they can shape this judicial development, profoundly. Most legislation addresses matter of public policy and leaves the judicial foundation and interpretation to the discretion of jurists. Sovereign authority usually lacks the time and resources to include the relevant legal rules and principles within the enactment of statutes and drafting of legislation, so those values are assumed and left to the discretion of the jurists who must consider them, when violated or challenged. Nonetheless, the sovereign retains the prerogative to override judicial interpretations of the law, but it must be exercised, deliberately, in order to accomplish this objective. That process is too cumbersome to be a regular occurrence, so the discretion of jurists within this matter remains an important feature of the common law system.

Jurists are not omnipotent, particular in terms of considering the wider implications of their decisions. Therefore, they frequently rely upon the advice of legal theorists and scholars, especially as provided within academic writing. Some of these authorities have assumed monumental reputations, such as the writings of Sir William Blackstone, the eminent eighteenth-century British jurist, or such prominent contemporary twentieth and twenty-first century scholars (including law professors, humanists, social scientists, and, even, natural scientists) as Ronald Dworkin, H. L. A. Hart, John Finnis, Richard Posner, John Rawls, Catharine MacKinnon, and Owen Hood Phillips. Scholarly sources frequently are cited by judges in support of their judicial opinions and interpretations of precedent, and their importance should not be undervalued. Nonetheless, this contribution generally complements precedent, rather than substituting for it.

Much of the law that is understood and applied by participants within the common law system is not necessarily found within a specific source, but is the product of, literally, centuries of common use, habit, shared practices, and legal assumptions consistent with the general tenor and theoretical comprehension of the common law. This knowledge is gained through the experiential process of becoming, and remaining, a legal practitioner, and it binds jurists together into a professional community that fulfills a fundamental need of, and obligation toward, their respective societies. The law is found within the interpretation and collective memory of the jurists, and the principle of *stare decisis* is just one expression (though the most prominent expression) of the common law as an institutional basis for a society's legal beliefs and operations.

Significance of the Common Law System

The peculiar isolation of England, its accelerated sense of national identity, and the political choices of its sovereign authority made the common law system, initially, a unique institutional expression of Western law and jurisprudence. The expanding influence of England (first, through the rest of Britain and its archipelago, including its union with Scotland, then through the British Empire, and finally, and indirectly, through its rebellious former colonies that became the United States) has made this system increasingly prominent, throughout the world. The common law system also provides an important source of appreciation for the idea of law, itself, as it has evolved within the Western tradition, especially considering the emphasis of judicial interpretation and its implications for evaluating the countries that employ this system and the respective legal traditions which this system serves.

The common law system remains less representative than the civil law system, though its popular representation (especially through the recent expansion of American film and its dramatic depictions of legal conflict) has had an enduring effect that should grow stronger, especially as the world continues to become more interactive. Growing economic and political cooperation requires increased legal interaction. Furthermore, knowledge of a country's legal system provides important clues to an understanding of its other legal norms and values. This factor is especially revealing when considering specific judicial rulings and the broader socio-economic, political, and legal contexts that these jurists feel compelled to address. Therefore, this traditional focus of comparative law has significant implications for the broader focus of law.

References

John Hamilton Baker, *The Common Law Tradition: Lawyers, Books, and the Law.* London, Hambledon, 2000.
Jerry Dupont, *The Common Law Abroad: Constitutional and Legal Legacy of the British Empire.* Littleton, CO, Rothman, 2001.
Palmer D. Evans, *Common Law Forms of Pleading and Practice.* Chicago, Callaghan, 1931.
Frederic William Maitland, *The Forms of Action at Common Law: A Course of Lectures*, A. H. Chaytor and W. J. Whittaker, eds. Cambridge, Cambridge University Press, 1971.
Sir Frederick Pollock, *The Law of Torts.* London, Stevens and Sons, 1916.
James W. Tubbs, *The Common Law Mind: Medieval and Early Modern Conceptions.* Baltimore, Johns Hopkins University Press, 2000.

CHAPTER 6

Civil Law Systems

The most prominent institutional legal system, by far, is the civil law system. Variations of its basic rules and structures can be found throughout the world, even within legal systems that should be institutionally distinctive, such as socialist legal systems. However, despite its ancient origins and Eurocentric features, it has proven to be highly adaptable to a variety of legal systems and cultures, particularly in terms of the flexibility it offers for the expression of fundamental political, economic, and social beliefs and values.

Historical Development of the Civil Law System

The historical origins of the current civil law system can be traced to ancient Rome. The republican period of Roman history was a time when values of order and discipline were particularly prized, owing to the tenuous position and vulnerability of the Roman city-state. Law became an effective instrument for uniting the Roman people, instructing them in their duties to each other and the republic, and ordering their general relationships. It was especially valuable to that period of Rome's history that fell under the guidance of the Roman Republic. The republican value of inclusiveness, in particular, was bolstered by the ideal of a law that united all of the various groups and classes of Rome, directed toward a common civic goal of survival and prosperity, especially through the control and regulation of their legal, political, social, and economic relationships.

Roman law provided a summation of legal principles. The *jus civile*, or "law of the city," was intended to be peculiar to the Romans, their experiences, their history, and their culture. The creation, and literal carving, of the twelve tables of the law (giving practical meaning to the concept of a law "written in stone") added a permanent, codified dimension to legal rules that summarized specific Roman principles. The advent of the Roman Empire, displacing the Roman Republic, instilled a strong sense of a universal mission into all fields of Rome's civic life, including the law. Among the Roman provinces, this process resulted in the previously described development of the *jus gentium*. But for Roman citizens, it heralded an even greater emphasis upon a Roman law that could unify, and define, the polity.

The interpretation of these laws continued to require a level of scholarly expertise, even under the empire. A heritage of such scholars, known as the "jurisconsults," arose, under the republic, and continued, under the empire, to provide this guidance. They received an intellectual training that sought to combine a broadly theoretical appreciation of Roman law and its link to its cultural heritage and the technical development of the edicts, codes, declarations, and other explicit expressions of the sovereign will of Rome. The writings of particularly prominent jurisconsults, such as Ulpian and Gaius, were maintained and emulated. They sought to provide a theoretically consistent outline to the various laws that emerged under this system. These writings were intended to be instructions for the practical application of law, while the actual laws retained their strict, permanent character.

Roman law also was intended to apply primarily to Roman citizens, since it reflected their particular culture and values. Non-Romans, including peoples subject to the military and political authority of the Roman state, maintained their own legal norms and practices in areas that did not directly affect the overriding Roman policy interests of maintaining peace and stability throughout its empire. But Rome, and all its citizens, were subject to laws they believed to be a reflection of more eternal truths, grounded in a rational system of thought and reflecting the superiority of a civilization that had, indeed, conquered the Mediterranean world.

Roman law continued to grow, as it accumulated imperial decrees, senatorial edicts, bureaucratic regulations, and the opinions of diverse, yet respected, scholars. Following the collapse of imperial authority in the Western Empire, the empire in the East (which would be called by later historians the Byzantine Empire) sought to preserve and revive the glory of ancient Rome, especially as it sought to reestablish its hegemony over the Mediterranean basin during the sixth and seventh centuries. One result of this political revival was the reorganization of Roman law, especially under Byzantine successors of the Roman Empire and particularly under the guidance of Emperor Justinian the Great.

The result of this desire, and the efforts it prompted, was the promulgation of the *Corpus Juris Civile*. Justinian wanted to recreate a legal unification for the Roman people, even if the capital had shifted to Constantinople. He commissioned leading jurisconsults and other legal scholars and civil officials to research the ancient Roman law and incorporate it into a reorganized effort that would be useful for the current, and future, Byzantine system. The result was a comprehensive written work that combined previous legal norms and statutes with an updated interpretation and organization. The *Corpus Juris Civile* consisted of four parts: the *Institutes*, consisting of a introduction to the basic principles and norms of Roman law, accessible to most educated people; the *Digests*, providing a detailed summary of Roman legal ideas and scholarship, especially as provided by the most prominent jurisconsults of Roman history; the *Codes*, which was a summary of all, still relevant Roman edicts, legislation, and other positive laws, from the origins of the city-state to the date of the commissioning of this project; the *Novels*, a section that would include all future legislation and ordinances.

This process provided order and stability to a tradition of Roman law that had become disorganized and unwieldy, especially given the political chaos that attended the demise of the Roman Empire in the West during the fourth and fifth centuries. This work was a considerable testament to the enduring image of Roman law and the institutional stability that it offered, but it was unable to persevere in the presence of the decentralization of economic, political, and social authority that was typical of the eventual collapse of all Roman authority and its displacement by the feudal system that symbolized the medieval period of European history. Local customs, the unwritten legal traditions of the tribal peoples who came to dominate Europe, and an inconsistent trend of blending these influences with the remnants of Roman legal authority, particularly regarding select areas of law (in which this sort of amalgamation proved convenient) became the norm, and the disciplined structure of Roman law, even as codified by Justinian, became a memory that was maintained only by scholars and the religious law of the Roman Catholic Church.

Canon law, and religious scholars who provided its theoretical expression, continued to provide this systematic model of a legal system. Otherwise, the customs of the feudal system and its legal norms prevailed. However, the gradual eroding of feudal authority and the lost dominance of the agrarian economy to the rising towns and mèrcantile economy provided an opportunity for the return of this ancient legal model. Equally gradually, increases in central authority and the emergence of the modern nation-state prompted a strong desire for sovereign authorities to benefit from a stable legal structure that could express this emerging national sentiment. Furthermore, a legal basis for dealing with the expanding economic, political, and social integration of Europe also increasingly was sought.

Consistent with the spirit of the Renaissance, European scholars began to ponder a "rebirth" of the law to parallel a perceived rebirth in the arts, politics, and social conditions, and they allowed themselves to be inspired by antiquity for that purpose. The University of Bologna became a prominent center for studying and promoting a revival of the Roman law that had been promulgated by Justinian for the Byzantines, several centuries previously. These scholars spread this intellectual approach throughout Europe, and it inspired a period of "reception" for the core principles of this interpretation of Roman law, particularly as a source of "common" legal values and institutions that all political authorities could accept and employ. This "common law," or *jus commune* (as distinct from the common law system evolving in England) became a foundation for the building of a comprehensive legal structure for each nation-state.

This adaptation of Roman law involved an interesting intellectual and practical process. The ancient text of the *Corpus Juris Civile* was explained and reconciled with modernizing trends and values through the efforts of scholars known as "glossators," because of their use of "glosses," or explanatory and summarizing comments provided within the margins of reprinted, edited versions of the *Corpus*. However, as a practical matter, the work of the glossators proved to be too literal and too tied to the ancient Roman context of this legal system to be truly useful for modern political authorities to adapt it as a practical legal model. Another group of scholars, known as the "commentators," or "post-glossators," subsequently emerged to provide interpretations and explanations of Roman law that could be reconciled with modern European ideas and needs within this area. This scholarly process created the conditions necessary for the practical adoption of this legal system by the maturing political societies of Europe, especially as they advanced their own goals of political centralization, in imitation of ancient precedents.

The civil law systems that were being developed within these modern nation-states were not consistent with each other. Each state sought to frame a legal structure that would meet its own particular needs, values, and goals. Roman law provided a unified model for legal reasoning and writing, while the study of the ancient *Corpus* offered concepts and principles that could provide the basis of supposedly "universal" legal norms. These ideas were supplemented by the development of commercial law, emerging from the various guilds and trade associations, that were based upon shared experiences and practical understandings of economic activity.

But this *jus commune* provided through this period of Roman law "reception" could not supply all of the content that these emerging political systems needed to address within their law, particularly as they sought to formulate areas of public law and, even, produce their own constitutional standards. Furthermore, the rise of humanism, especially during the seventeenth and eighteenth centuries, shifted emphasis away from the supposedly ubiquitous model of the Roman law toward the tendency to treat even comprehensive works like the *Corpus Juris Civile* as mere historical documents, reflecting the mores of a particular time, place, and culture.

Therefore, while the structure of Roman law continued to offer a useful format, and the methods of legal teaching and reasoning arising from the example of the University of Bologna united European jurists and other legal and political elites, a shift of focus occurred toward the formulation of a civil law content that would reflect the legal ideals and political values of each nation-state.

One method for achieving this goal was codification. Initially, the precepts of this civil law tradition could be transmitted and followed through the formal apprehension of rules and principles established by the universities that trained and educated a society's legal practitioners. But codification, modeled loosely upon the codes of the *Corpus*, could provide an even more permanent source of law that would ensure consistency of interpretation and application throughout the legal system. The systematic theoretical efforts of Dutch legal scholars of the seventeenth century (ironically related to the modern cultivation of natural law theory and its attempt to express universal and transhistorical legal ideals) prompted the construction of a comprehensive legal system within that society that presaged the advent of civil law codification.

This system of codification would become so pervasive that the contemporary observers occasionally refer to the civil law system as the "code law" system. The French Revolution was the most immediate context for this occurrence. The First Consul, Napoléon Bonaparte (soon to be crowned Emperor Napoléon I) arranged this codification by assembling a small commission of eminent French jurists who constructed a legal system for France, at the start of the nineteenth century, that was not a restatement of law but, rather, a new pronouncement of French legal values, emphasizing the predominant position of private property, contracts, traditional patriarchy, and the unifying proposition of equality before the law. It articulated these principles within codes that were systematically organized and categorized into five books (civil code, commercial code, penal code, civil procedure, criminal procedure), each addressing a fundamental area of law and its implementation. This method of organization was an important contribution of the Roman model.

The French civil code (later popularly called the *Code Napoléon*) was written in a style that could be comprehensive yet, also, accessible. It emulated the traditional Roman emphasis upon human reason as a source for interpreting law, so its separate codes were expressed in general terms that could be understood and applied, by all educated people, to a variety of events and conditions. It combined the universal truths supposedly advanced by the reception of the *jus commune* with the national goals and "universal" revolutionary values of modern France. It also committed this law to a written format that would displace previous versions, offer an unambiguous and consistent expression, and be knowable to all persons. Thus it imposed upon governments, jurists, and ordinary people, alike, strict uniformity upon its interpretation and application.

The *Code Napoléon* served as a model for a modern civil law system that was widely imitated. However, toward the end of the nineteenth century, an alternative approach to the civil law system was produced in the newly unified nation-state of Germany. The desire to promote and define German national identity in the wake of a history of decentralized German political entities that had been brought together only recently strengthened an impetus that already had existed among German jurists and legal scholars. The civil law structure provided by the Roman law offered a good framework, but the intellectual approach of the French model seemed insufficient for achieving a German law for a German people.

The leading scholarly impetus for the development of the German civil law was a movement known as the Historical School, led by the eminent legal scholar, Friedrich Carl von Savigny. He stressed the belief that law was like all other expressions of a people, so it should not be derived from a search for abstract principles but from historical and cultural analysis. The scholarly development of a German civil law that he inspired, known as the *usus modernus pandectarum*, resulted in the "pandectist" style of civil law. This approach found inspiration within the pragmatism that had motivated the original development of Roman legal traditions, and it sought to create legal codes and principles that were derived from German legal and cultural history and would be directly relevant to the political, social, and cultural expectations and habits of a distinctly German society and its people. Antecedents to the modern German law, such as the Prussian Land Law of the eighteenth century, contributed to this adaptation.

Interestingly, the pandectists who drafted the German civil codes would adopt a formalism that often would become increasingly abstract and would ignore important aspects of German cultural, social, and economic ideals. One of the most conspicuous features of this code was the first book, known as the General Part, which provides essential conceptual definitions and general principles of the law in impressive depth and scope, and which is intended to be used for interpreting the other codes. But the result is not as accessible as the *Code Napoléon*, for it is even more detailed, technical, and intended for the expert practitioner. It also tended to be more precise and pervasive, attempting to account for all possible legal situations and relationships and establishing strict and detailed instructions for their resolution. It has provided a legal "science" that is intended to address the particular needs and expectations of an evolved German society that ultimately is the product of its unique history.

Although other variations exist (especially within societies that have a "mixed" system that includes both common law and civil law institutions), the French and German models of the civil law, especially in terms of the constructions of their respective civil codes, have been the most prominent influences for other legal systems, throughout the world. The clearly identifiable structural features of the civil law have made it particularly useful for political systems seeking to create their own law and jurisprudence. Civil law has continued to evolve during the twentieth and twenty-first centuries (especially the pandectist model), but its essential features have assumed lasting characteristics that are a product of its historical evolution and the inspiration of its ancient Roman origins. These features include enormous variations, but the underlying principles and institutional assumptions remain recognizable, despite this variety. These areas of basic affinity should be emphasized, while acknowledging the potential for considerable divergence.

Structure and Practices of the Judicial System

The structural outline of civil law systems differ considerably from the common law system. A good illustration of the essential difference can be found through the labeling of the civil law as an "inquisitorial" system, in contrast to the description of the common law as an "accusatorial" system. Some commentators object to the use of this term, because of the concern that it will suggest an association with the notorious image of the brutality of the Roman Catholic Inquisition of the medieval and early modern periods. However, a more proper explanation of this label suggests that a civil law system creates a judicial environment that encourages a search for truth as the true purpose of law, rather than the common law image of a contest between opposing forces that want to persuade a jury of the superiority of its subjective interpretation of the truth.

Civil law courts are the culmination of this "inquiry" into legal truth. Certain participants within the process do bring a particular motive or perspective to the proceedings: legal practitioners representing the government, for example, are convinced of the guilt of an accused person, while that person's legal representative may be equally persuaded of that person's innocence. However, the process, itself, is designed to be a collective and cooperative effort among judicial and law enforcement professionals. Judges do not serve, therefore, as neutral arbiters of the process but as active participants who direct this inquisitorial search for legal truth, but this aspect of the civil law system will be addressed within the context of its procedural and structural characteristics.

Meanwhile, an institutional description of the judicial system, its structure, and its organization reveals other important and interesting contrasts between the civil law and common law systems. While geography generally is a determining factor regarding a particular jurisdiction, the nature of the issue or controversy can be even more pertinent. Common law courts generally are comprehensive, in the sense that all legal disputes are subject to the jurisdiction of the same court, with a few exceptions (especially regarding administrative law) that are, nonetheless, subject to the unifying authority of the same higher courts. Civil law courts tend to be more highly specialized, though, according to the category of legal issue that is being addressed.

Most criminal, and many civil, matters are addressed by a category of court often labeled an "ordinary court." However, in addition to ordinary courts, other courts can exist that are devoted exclusively to other legal areas, including family law courts, commercial law courts, labor law courts, and equity courts. More significantly, these courts are not brought together under a unified appellate system, but often have, instead, their own, specialized appellate courts, with separate final courts of appeal that have jurisdiction exclusively over their own area of law. This distinction might seem subtle, because of selective examples of specialization that also occur within the common law system and the fact that appeals of most criminal, and many civil, disputes within some civil law systems often are subject to the ultimate authority of the same final court of appeal, although these courts often are further divided into specialized divisions that separately consider appeals of exclusive categories of law. But the emphasis upon a more parochial, rather than a generalized, approach to legal organization and expertise is the feature of most civil law systems that is truly indicative of the more significant distinctions between the two systems.

Courts of original jurisdiction consider matters of both "fact" and "law," just like the same courts within a common law system. However, unlike the appellate courts of a common law system, the appeal courts of a civil law system generally are empowered to review all aspects of an appealed decision. These judges are not confined to considering controversies regarding the interpretation of legal rules and principles but also may reevaluate evidence. This distinction is related to other themes that are integral to the civil law system as a whole.

The tendency toward separate hierarchies of courts within a civil law system reflects the influence of the organization of law, itself, especially as found within civil codes. Administrative tribunals exist within most common law systems, but the decisions of these tribunals are subject to the same appellate authority as the conventional courts, with their geographically determined jurisdictions and comprehensive authority over both criminal and civil matters. Civil law systems have their own administrative court structures, independent from other court structures within the same system. This theme of specialization and the general lack of a single high court of final appeal for the entire system (though that factor does not preclude an ability to provide a unified oversight of the entire system) is one that is better understood in connection with other procedural, organizational, and conceptual features of the civil law system.

Legal Education and Training

Specialization and formal education are consistent features of a civil law system. Superficially, the process of becoming a legal practitioner within a civil law system resembles the process that has evolved within the common law system. However, the historical origins of the professional accreditation process for the two systems are very distinct, and the underlying themes associated with them are even more indicative of broader differences between the two legal systems. In particular, the distinction indicates a contrasting stress between the experienced-based nature of the common law system and the formal, scholastic emphasis of the civil law system.

The modern European reception of Roman law was a product of the expanding universities, beginning with the University of Bologna. That heritage is continued within civil law countries, which insist that its legal practitioners receive a university degree in law, prior to being eligible to be certified as qualified to serve within this profession. The common law countries now generally require their lawyers to have university degrees and, in some countries, the law degree is earned as a professional degree that follows an academic baccalaureate. However, the overwhelming emphasis for a common law system rests with the professional society, distinct from colleges and universities, that require applicants to enter their profession to demonstrate their practical legal knowledge and acquired abilities in law through an examination, typically known as the "bar exam."

Civil law countries frequently require an examination, following the university degree process, to certify its legal practitioners. However, the emphasis remains upon the formal education process as the most significant part of the path toward becoming a law professional. Furthermore, while the "law schools" of common law systems prepare lawyers to be generalists (and the "pre-law" undergraduate experience, within the countries where it exists, typically do not offer law as an academic major), universities of civil law countries require their students to choose a specialized area of law to study. These students typically receive a degree within this area of legal specialty, which becomes the basis for their subsequent certification as legal professionals.

Civil law systems do not, as a rule, have a single, generic category of "lawyer" that exists within common law systems. The French system, for example, divides professional legal responsibility among different practitioners, such as the *avocats* (who generally participate directly within court proceedings), *avoués* (who provide specific legal services to clients), *conseils juridiques* (who serve as legal consultants), and *notaires* (responsible for drafting and maintaining important contractual, and other, documents, including evidentiary items), each of whom provide parochial legal functions that may not be exercised by other categories of legal professionals. Not all civil law systems are as highly compartmentalized as France, but they generally are much more specialized than common law systems.

These practitioners focus upon their particular fields within their university programs, although it is the process of post-university certification and internship that is properly responsible for making that actual distinction. Another such area of expertise is the legal profession of being a judge. Common law judges are appointed upon the basis of their abilities and experience, and they occupy an extremely prestigious place, both within the legal hierarchy and within society. Judges within civil law systems generally are regarded as civil servants, performing a largely bureaucratic, though extremely important, function. They are trained to administer the law, rather than preside over it. Furthermore, they do not shape the law through the interpretive process of precedent, and their status is a direct consequence of the nature of the system.

The role of the legal scholar bears more directly upon the practical functioning of the civil law system than it does upon the operation of the common law system. Scholars often are responsible for creating and shaping the very "doctrine" of law (as it is formally known) and jurisprudence that is the foundation of the civil law. They are the teachers of other professionals, they generally dominate the commissions that draft the codes, and their theoretical writings provide an extremely important resource for clarifying ambiguities or engaging in other exercises of interpreting the meaning and application of the law. Furthermore, they are not just narrow legal specialists but include scholars from many other fields that influence, or are affected by, the law, especially within the social sciences.

The role of legal scholars, as distinct from lawyers, becomes particularly important within the area of constitutional law. Ultimately, this distinction is a defining part of the mosaic that constitutes the civil law system. The formal education that shapes these professionals also reflects the system, its themes, and its values, as revealed by other institutional features of the civil law.

Legal Procedures and Structures

A common fallacy is the claim (made, particularly, by observers who live within common law countries) that persons accused of a crime within a common law system are presumed innocent until proven guilty, while the opposite assumption exists within a civil law system, placing a burden upon the court to determine an accused person's guilt. Part of the reason for that perception may stem from an emphasis upon the nature of the courtroom procedures of the judicial process. But, in fact, the courtroom proceedings, or "trial," of a civil law system really is only a phase of the broader trial process. By the time an accused person has reached that stage of the criminal process, a great deal of evaluation regarding their guilt or innocence already has occurred. A similar condition exists respecting civil and administrative judicial proceedings.

Prior to the courtroom phase, an accused person or the parties in a civil case are subjected to a "pre-trial" phase. Persons experienced in the common law system associate the term "pre-trial" with a certain preliminary agenda of matters that must be administratively addressed before a trial actually can commence, such as the arraignment, when the accused person enters a formal plea and the trial is scheduled, or the "discovery" process, in which certain evidence is shared, particularly by the prosecution with the defense. However, the pre-trial phase of a civil law judicial process is a relatively lengthy, formal process of evidentiary evaluation. Usually, judges play a leading, and very active, role in this process, and the legal counsel of the government, the accused person, or parties to a civil controversy also are active participants, along with relevant police officers or other criminal justice professionals. All available evidence is examined, and even the crime scene will be visited. The evaluation of the case made against the accused person or the party named in a suit is considered extremely critically, especially by the judges, during this phase.

Generally, if the evidence does not suggest that a strong case exists against an accused person, or that a plaintiff does not have sufficient grounds for making a claim against the defense, the process will be terminated. Therefore, especially within a criminal case, a preponderance of evidence and other indications need to exist to warrant a continuation of the judicial process, and a failure to meet that standard should result in the dismissal of the charges. The evidence necessary for commencing a trial within a common law system, however, generally does not rise to that level of indication, except in cases in which the indictment of a separate judicial body, known as a "grand jury," is involved. A shortage of convincing evidence can result in a dismissal of charges or a suit within a common law process, but usually only once the trial phase actually begins.

A determination that sufficient evidence exists to suggest that an accusation is both valid and provable often results, in criminal proceedings, in an accused person seeking some sort of "deal" regarding punishment, or, in civil proceedings, in the defendant seeking to negotiate a settlement. However, such a determination, made during the pre-trial phase of a civil law judicial process, is not definitive, and a defendant retains the legal option to proceed to the formal courtroom phase, conventionally known as the "trial" phase. Since a considerable body of evidence already has been evaluated and accepted, prior to this stage of the process being reached, a preponderance of guilt or liability already has been demonstrated (though not yet conclusively), so it is not surprising that an assumption that the defendant is guilty and must challenge the evidence to prove innocence might tend to prevail, especially among the public. However, criminal defendants may not be convicted until their guilt has been proven, convincingly, nor may plaintiffs prevail until they achieve a higher level of evidentiary proof than the pre-trial stage normally reveals.

The trial phase also reveals the "inquisitorial" nature of the civil law system. Judges are active participants in the process of questioning witnesses, challenging evidence, and considering the claims of both accusers and accused. Counsel representing the government, which makes the accusation in a criminal case, often is not as overtly partisan as government lawyers in a criminal trial within a common law system. All parties participate in the "search for truth," resulting in a trial that can seem more like a formalized investigation than a legal contest. The fact that all parties generally enjoy unlimited access to all evidence, even when acquired by other parties (also known as an unlimited "right of discovery") further promotes this tone.

The final determination is made by judges, who having ultimate authority over both an evaluation of the "facts" (the evidence and its applicability to a particular case) and the interpretation of the "law," including relevant statutes, rules of procedure, and other considerations. Occasionally, a civil law system may make a provision of a limited role for lay juries, but it clearly is the exception. Usually, the trial includes a panel of judges (with the most senior one playing the most prominent procedural role) who determine the outcome by a majority vote. However, their determination is not, necessarily, final.

The ruling of the trial judges may be appealed by any party—including the government, should a defendant be determined to be innocent of the charges. The possibility that an appeal court will overrule the decision made during the trial phase tends to be far less likely than it is within a common law system. Judges generally have little discretion, particularly because of the specificity of the codes and other sources of legal terms and principles they are trained to follow. Even the specific remedies (such as criminal penalties or damage awards) usually are determined by a strict formula that is specified within the penal codes or through a doctrinal method. Still, the guidance of the legal system is not absolute, and gaps can arise, particularly regarding specific applications to particular circumstances. Such disparities may be subject to the discretion of the judges, and the conclusions of appellate judges may differ with the interpretation offered. Furthermore, a judicial ruling could have an effect upon public policy that needs to be reconciled.

Traditionally, the appeal court will only consider the law, rather than the facts, but that restriction is not always observed. Additional appeals may be to higher appellate courts, including the final court for determining cases within a particular judicial area. Generally, though, the civil law system tends to discourage judicial discretion in favor of a relatively definitive body of legal rules, ideas, and principles. This factor, ultimately, provides the true foundation for the civil law system.

Sources of Law

The most conspicuous source of legal rules, ideas, and principles within the civil law system generally are its codes. Commissions of scholars and other legal experts, rather than the legal opinions and practices of previous jurists, are the originators of these codes. Codes, unlike precedents, are not cumulative; when new codes are promulgated, the codes they have replaced become obsolete. They are sanctioned by the sovereign and organized according to the various substantive and procedural areas that constitute the body of law. The detailed, cross-referenced descriptions and formulas of hundreds of separate codes leave little, if any, interpretative ambiguity. They enforce a uniform standard of law, its understanding, and its application.

Judges are trained to administer the law, rather than truly explicate its meaning. They receive instruction regarding uniform methods of review and application, as sanctioned by universities which, in turn, conform to a single, accepted standard. In the absence of formal codes, a civil law system may provide, through its universities, a comprehensive doctrine of these rules, ideas, and principles that are intended to be understood and followed just as stringently and uniformly as if they were contained in a positive body of written directions.

Scholarly writings, widely accepted by the legal community of a civil law society, supplement the codes, particularly providing an interpretive "doctrine." Judges and other legal practitioners are expected to be guided by this doctrine in matters of legal ambiguity and silence. Since scholarly agreement does not normally offer the consistency of a single body of codes, only a limited discretion in understanding and applying the writings provided by selected scholars normally is available for judges. Occasionally, recourse even might be taken to a limited reference to other, similar rulings. Therefore, both variation and disagreement is possible, in this respect, so an absence of judicial controversy remains inescapable.

The command of the sovereign can change the codes and its ideas. It also provides legislation and policy, which is presumed to be consistent with the rules and principles of the codes. Therefore, judges and other legal practitioners are expected to reconcile legislation and policy with the law, even if it requires a new interpretation of accepted legal norms. Again, the civil law system can never be so rigid that it precludes all variation. Nonetheless, it remains much more immutable, in theory *and* practice, than the common law system often provides.

Significance of the Civil Law System

The civil law system is neither better or worse than its common law alternative; it simply serves a different historical and cultural requirement. Its tendency to deny interpretive discretion to legal elites offers a particularly interesting contrast, and it suggests a higher level of deference to the sovereign's ultimate authority over the law, including a democratic sovereign. Certain institutional advantages of the civil law seem to make it more readily adaptable as an institutional means of legal expression. Clearly, many other societies, including emerging nation-states, have adopted the civil law as their preferred system. However, numerous variations upon this system exist, so it is very difficult to explain the civil law in terms of a "typical" example or description.

Nonetheless, important themes predominate, and the civil law system offers an institutional ideal that has been emulated by the vast majority of the world's societies. It offers an especially good system (though not the only one) for expressing the overarching principles and values of law. Its structural role should be emphasized, particularly, in terms of that perspective. Both the common law and civil law systems offer a frame, in that respect, for the more pervasive mosaic of law.

References

James G. Apple and Robert P. Deyling, *A Primer on the Civil-Law System*. Washington, Federal Judicial Center, 1995.
Sir George Bowyer, *Introduction to the Study and Use of the Civil Law*. London, Stevens, 1874.
Edward L. Glaeser, *Legal Origins*. Cambridge, MA, National Bureau of Economic Research, 2001.
John Henry Merryman, David S. Clark, and John O. Haley, *The Civil Law Tradition: Europe, Latin America, and East Asia*. Charlottesville, VA, Michie, 1994.
Peter Stein, *Roman Law in European History*. Cambridge, Cambridge University Press, 1999.
Arthur Taylor Von Mehren, *The Civil Law System: Cases and Materials for the Comparative Study of Law*. Boston, Little, Brown, 1977.

CHAPTER 7

Western Religion and Its Law

Unlike much of the Eastern religious heritage, Western religions tend to be distinguished from other areas of society, including politics, economics, ideology, and law. Nonetheless, many of the beliefs and values expressed through the theological pronouncements and practices of the major Western religions parallel developments in other areas and institutions. Often, these beliefs and values have actually played a significant role in shaping these other aspects of Western life.

That influence is revealed through a comparison of both the religious and secular heritages of law within the broader Western tradition. Therefore, an examination of the legal traditions of Western religions is both useful and important for appreciating Western law and its worldwide legacy. The three most important religious traditions also share certain common bonds and origins, yet they express law in profoundly different ways that can be related to equally contrasting secular approaches to law. The largest of these religions is Roman Catholic Christianity.

Catholicism and the Canon Law

The formal emergence of law within Christianity was a product of its interaction with the Roman Empire, of which it eventually became the official state religion. Prior to that emergence, the instruction of Jewish texts (including the Hebrew scriptures of the Bible), as well as the transmitted teachings of Jesus and his disciples (especially St. Paul of Tarsus), served that purpose for Christians and their religious leaders. But, as a "universal," or *catholic* consciousness arose among the dominant Christian community whose allegiance lay with the Bishop of Rome (later known as the Pope), the need to express a unifying body of doctrine and guidance made this formal legal expression an increasing priority. The eventual result of this recognition was the organization of the law of the church into a series of definitive declarations, known as "canons." This legal model also has been adopted within Orthodox and Anglican Christianity, but the Roman Catholic example is particularly prominent, especially as an influence for later secular developments.

The codification of the laws of the church into a series of canons clearly seems to have emulated the example of Roman law, which provided the secular authority for nearly all members of this denomination of Christianity that would become known as Roman Catholicism. Other features of the canon law also suggest this affinity, including the detailed nature of these canons, the lack of discretion permitted for their substantive interpretation, and the ultimate reliance upon recognized scholars for providing the doctrinal guidance for the practical application of the canons. Certain themes emerge, as confirmed by theological explanations, regarding the canon law as it has been received, the most prominent being the advancement of religious unity, the promotion of church authority, the imposition of moral duties, and the elucidating role of a *teleological* method for revealing and fulfilling this law.

These themes are consistent with the broader Western tradition of natural law. Indeed, Roman Catholic theology has been strongly influenced by, and has equally influenced the development of, this natural law heritage. The theme of "unity" suggests the universal and transhistorical emphasis of natural law, as found through the structure that emerged for this denomination. The theme of "authority" bears a relationship to the previous theme, although it also suggests the stress upon obedience that has been prominent within Roman Catholic theology. Ironically, it also can be related to the later, secular concept of sovereignty that led to the displacement of natural law theory with legal positivism and the civil law system that would promote this concept. The theme of "duty" clearly relates to the *deontological* principle of natural law, particularly in terms of the attention the canon law devotes to all aspects of the lives of faithful members of the church, including such matters as charity, family obligations, and human sexuality. The *teleological* theme is one that was introduced at a later period, relating to the reintroduction of, and perceived competition from, the writings of Aristotle throughout Europe, especially during the twelfth and thirteenth centuries.

Aristotle insisted upon evaluating all things according to their conformity to their ultimate purpose, or "end," as designated by the Greek word *telos*. The response of medieval Christian scholarship to this aspect of Aristotle's empirical model of evaluation was a claim that, since all things are created by God and are reflections of God's will, all things should seek to fulfill the purpose of God's universal plan. In that way, all attitudes and behavior consistent with the apparent ultimate purpose, or *telos*, of a person, thing, or activity lead, ultimately, toward God. Canon law adjusted to this idea, applying this modified Aristotelian idea (especially as illuminated by St. Thomas Aquinas) to all areas of existence, such as the subject of human sexuality.

Canon law has specified that the ultimate *telos* of human sexuality is procreation. Therefore, sexual activity should be directed toward that proper "end." Furthermore, the *deontological* requirement imposed by the canons actually make the process of having sex, within marriage, a moral duty, rather than an option. The relationship between the natural law tradition and canon law is affirmed through this approach, and it is indicative of all of the themes relating to it, as well as the general tenor of this sort of religious legal model. Furthermore, it provides insight into certain secular legal norms that parallel this religious standard.

The formal sources of canon law are derived from that theme of "authority." They are not discovered by people, but transmitted and translated by the church. Therefore, even St. Thomas Aquinas' category of "divine law," which is provided directly from God (such as the Ten Commandments or the Sermon on the Mount) may not be received directly, but only after the precepts of this divine law have been explained and expounded by the church as the authoritative intermediary. Despite the theme of "unity," more than one conduit can be found for promulgating the canons, although the Pope retains ultimate authority over their maintenance and enforcement.

The most prominent source of canon law has been the official proclamations emanating from ecumenical councils, which have been convened, intermittently, throughout the church's history. They are intended to symbolize the community the church, as a whole, through inclusion of representatives of the clergy, church theologians, the laity, in addition to the church hierarchy and the Pope. Therefore, the perceived strength of this authority is particularly strong, as demonstrated by the sweeping changes in canon law (especially in terms of the canons governing the Mass and other liturgy) introduced as a result of the Second Vatican Council, which concluded in 1963.

The Pope may, upon his sole authority, make changes to canon law. Ironically, this authority was affirmed by another ecumenical council, the First Vatican Council, which concluded in 1870. When making a pronouncement *ex cathedra* (literally, from the chair, or, figuratively, from his official "seat" of office), the Pope's rulings on faith and morals are regarded as being "infallible" and, thus, beyond challenge. The concept of law as an expression of sovereign will is revealed, again, through this use of overarching authority, even though it has been exercised only sparingly.

Finally, as thorough as the drafters of the canons attempt to be, interpretive gaps remain that cannot be filled solely through papal authority. Consistent with the workings of the secular civil law system, these gaps may be remedied through the writings of theologians who serve as official commentators. They play a role similar to the Roman law glossators and commentators, and their comments generally are found alongside the published canons. Separate theological writings also serve that purpose, and the writings of St. Thomas Aquinas (especially as found within his monumental treatise *Summa Theologicæ*) offers the most conspicuous example of this contribution to canon law. Gratian's reorganization of canon law was an attempt to make this process, and the canons, themselves, more systemic and orderly. A "science" of canon law thus has been developed, not unlike John Austin's "scientific" approach to legal positivism, as described within a previous chapter. This process has been advanced by (in addition to the glossators and commentators) church legal scholars known as the "decretists" and "decratalists," who have offered critical commentary on Gratian's *Decretal* and other, similar collections, respectively. This category of "decretal" is borrowed from the tradition of Roman law, and it consists of papal decrees, in the form of answers to the theological and institutional questions of bishops and other church authorities. Along with this decretal law and the contributions of church scholars and theologians, the canons are organized according to the categories of counciliar law that emerges from councils, the proclamations *ex cathedra*, and earlier sources that can be traced to the origins of the church.

The canons are organized into seven "books," each corresponding to a different subject matter, such as family law, liturgical matters, and church sacraments. Collectively, these canons are placed with the *Codex Juris Canonici* of 1917 and 1983, and its more than 1,700 canons are regarded as guides, and not just prohibitions, for over a billion Roman Catholics, throughout the world. Similarities between canon law and secular civil law reflect a similarity of origins and a mutual reinforcement of ideals and structure. Therefore, a critical appreciation of the canon law of Roman Catholicism (as well as the canon law of other denominations, particularly of the Anglican and Eastern Orthodox varieties) offer an important source for comparative legal analysis.

Judaism and the *Talmud*

The expression of religious belief through the promulgation, interpretation, and implementation of the law is a foundational feature of Judaism, which is, in turn, the foundation of a general Western religious heritage. The central expression of this law is found within the *Talmud*, which consists of sixty-three books that originated with a transcription of the oral law which was, in turn, derived from augmentations and extensions of the first five books of the Bible (called the *Torah*) to human existence. The *Talmud* includes the decisions of recognized scholarly authorities, particularly *rabbis*, and current authorities are expected to refer to these earlier decisions, prior to offering further interpretation or modification of the law. This cumulative record, therefore, roughly resembles the underlying premise of *stare decisis* found within the common law system.

The *Torah* represents the recorded word of God. The *Talmud* represents the written human commentary and explanation of the word of God. It began with an initial transcription of oral legal traditions, finished during the second century CE (called the *Mishnah*) referring to the "repeated study" of principal religious requirements and guidelines that had become the focus of Jewish religious life. The *Mishnah* is divided into six "orders," according to subject matter.

But a much larger commentary upon the *Mishnah*, called the *Gemara*, or "completion," gradually was added to the *Talmud*. The *Gemara* was completed three centuries later, and it consists of two, separate works, the Palestinian and the Babylonian; the latter work is larger and regarded, generally, as the more authoritative part. Additionally, a separate body of commentaries upon the *Torah*, called the *Midrash*, supplements the *Talmud*, although it is not, technically, part of it. Nonetheless, it is consistent with the composite structure of Jewish law that is one of the most notable features that seems to be epitomized by the *Talmud*.

Two broad subject areas are discerned within the *Torah*, and they define the emphasis of the *Talmud*. The first category, *halakha*, addresses legal and doctrinal matters, while the second category, *haggada*, deals with practical issues of daily life, particularly factors that are not strictly legal in nature. But it is the actual format of the *Talmud*, rather than its subject matter, that is especially fascinating from a comparative legal perspective. The laws are organized in a manner that allows for immediate cross-referencing to the comments that interpret, and expand upon, them. Some of these comments immediately follow the main passage, much like the notes found within the written text of a common law decision. Other comments are placed within the margins, much like the notes upon the Roman law provided by the glossators. The effect is a main text, surrounded by a variety of interpretive text, offering a mosaic of understanding. This variety of interpretive comments can be confusing, so it is considered imperative that the *Talmud* be subject to the ongoing translation and application of current scholars, particularly the *rabbis*, who are trained to perform that task, especially for the benefit of all practicing Jews.

This tradition of scholarly approaches is encapsulated by the *zugots*, identified historically as five pairs of prominent Jewish legal scholars who offered contrasting methods and perspectives for interpreting the *Talmud*. The most famous *zugots* founded interpretive schools that have not only dominated Jewish religious legal thought, but who also provide a fascinating insight into a general comparative understanding of legal interpretation and a common conflict that arises concerning the interpretation of any legal idea. These *zugots* were, roughly, contemporaries who differed sharply in their respective approaches to the *Torah*. They lived during the first century CE, so they predate the drafting of the *Talmud*, but they established an important oral tradition of the law that became highly influential toward the eventual development of the Talmud.

The first of these two *zugots* was Shammai. He believed that a literal interpretation of the received law should prevail. He objected to human attempts to modify the word of God and believed this presumption could be avoided only by a dutiful attempt to discern God's genuine will and intent; otherwise, the result would be a proud and arrogant attempt by humans to substitute their own judgment for the infinite wisdom of their creator. Furthermore, he distinctly cautioned against the attempts of well educated persons to offer such guidance, for they might impose their personal beliefs upon the whole people, thus undermining the collective heritage that the received word of God is intended to provide them, especially in terms of becoming a true community.

A contrast to this interpretive approach was offered by Hillel, who, according to some accounts, may actually have influenced the boyhood instruction of Jesus in the meaning of the Jewish law. Hillel believed that the law should be adapted to changing circumstances. God confers this capacity for intellectual and practical adaptation upon the people, so it is not unexpected that they should employ it. The spirit of the received word must be respected, but attempts to apply it literally could pervert that spirit and intent. The law, as received by previous generations, was constructed in a way that was most suitable for their historical context; it would be inappropriate to impose the interpretation that arises from those circumstances of a past generation upon the needs and aspirations of a living people. Therefore, a literal interpretation, ironically, can pervert the higher meaning and purpose of the law.

This divergence between Shammai and Hillel and the interpretive schools they inspired is indicative of the ongoing diversity that is available to the reception and application of Jewish law. It also is interesting from a comparative perspective, for the debate between jurists who insist upon upholding a literal interpretation of law, as opposed to jurists who assert, with equal vehemence, the need to adapt the law to the conditions, values, and other circumstances of the community that actually is affected by it, is indicative of a disputation that also occurs within secular legal systems. Indeed, this division is especially apparent within common law systems, especially in relation to the interpretation of public law.

The *Talmud* provides both restrictions and guidance for the Jewish people. It serves a primarily religious purpose, yet it reveals many ideas and techniques that have become part of the development of Western secular law, too. This influence of religious legal norms and practices especially is apparent in the areas of legal analysis and operation. It also is revealed within the legal tradition of the yet another great Western religion that emerged at a later date.

Islam and *Shari'a*

The most prominent theme of Islamic law (particularly law as developed within the *Sunni* tradition, which is the most dominant Islamic denomination) could be cited, arguably, as the concept of "consensus." This theme has additional significance through the added requirement that, once a consensus of legal analysis is achieved, future variations of interpretation are not permitted. Therefore, the law is intended to promote the unity of a religious community through this expression of faith and obedience to God.

Islamic law is called *Shari'a*, which roughly translates as "the clear path that must be followed." This path is established through consensus, in addition to other important themes. The law should not adapt itself to human affairs; instead, the world must adapt to the eternal truths revealed by the law. This theme complements another theme concerning the imposition of the law upon human conduct. Strictly speaking, human actions do not conform to, or transgress, the law. Actions are regarded, instead, as being *mandub* ("praiseworthy") or *makruh* ("blameworthy"), so the law provides a context for evaluating human choices, rather than a mere system of precise prescriptions and prohibitions. This theme is consistent with the thematic understanding of *Shari'a* as a process of discovery. It is a search for the legal guidance provided by God, especially as revealed by the prophet Mohammed and through the sacred scripture of God. The most important source is the *Qur'an* (also spelled *Koran*), communicated to Mohammed by God and referring to the higher truths of the universe that serve as the ultimate source of law.

The science of Islamic law, known as the *fiqh*, is directed toward a revelation of legal truths, rather than their development. The ultimate source for the law comes, therefore, from the *Qur'an*. However, since the *Qur'an* does not address every area that the law affects, it is supplemented, for Sunni Moslems, by the *Sunna*, which provides accounts of the lifestyle and practices of Mohammed. The *Sunna* consists of the collected traditions of the actions and statements of Mohammed, known as the *hadith*. These traditions were transmitted, for centuries, by successors to Mohammed, until the research of dominant scholars (especially Bukārī and Muslim), designated as doctors of Islam, verified the authenticity of the *hadith*.

This work of the doctors of Islam is the key source of the modern knowledge of Islamic law and theology. Current legal scholars of *Shari'a*, known as the *fukahā*, merely discover and transmit this already established understanding of the law. The consensus of the community is established through them and applied by Islamic judges, or *kādī*. It is not based upon a shared agreement of all members of the faith, but upon their recognized religious and legal leaders. That agreement, furthermore, does not involve formulation or evolution of the law, but merely its revelation and application, as provided by God, through Mohammed and, later, the work of the doctors of Islam.

The legal consensus reached is intended to be a unanimous one, and it is achieved through a result called *ijmā*. The attainment of *ijmā* results from a process called *ijtihad*, which proceeds from one technique to another, until a unity of opinion can be agreed. It often is employed in pursuit of the reconciliation of a practical problem with a religiously based solution. The first step is the consultation of the *Qur'an*. If the *Qur'an* offers clear guidance, there is no need to proceed, further. However, if the *Qur'an* appears to be silent or vague on the matter, then the truth is sought through an examination of the *Sunna*.

A failure to arrive at a solution at that point may necessitate recourse to an analytical technique known as *qiyas*, which involves the application of subsidiary principles of reasoning. Two options available as methods of reasoning include *istihsan*, which emphasizes equitable preference (especially in terms of a general desire to provide for fairness to all members of the community), and *istislah*, which considers the affect of a decision upon the interests of the community. This second method can be particularly important when applying *Shari'a* to a particular society or political system, in addition to using it for the purpose of discovering the proper method of interpreting and applying the will of God toward contemporary matters that find no direct reference within the *Qur'an* or the *Sunna*. Once these evaluative methods have been employed, the results need to be reconciled among the different, recognized authorities, in order to achieve the sort of consensus necessary for the unity imposed by *ijma*.

This final evaluation rests upon two considerations. *Zann*, or "conjecture," is a tentative conclusion, because it is based upon the finding of a single *kādī* or a small group of scholars. *Yaqin*, or "certainty," occurs when a consensus, in support of interpretive unity, is demonstrated. While *yaqin* remains the obvious goal of *ijmā*, it often does not remain undisputed. Part of this lack of practical unity is the product of the diversity within Islam, itself. Different schools of interpretation, known as *madhhab* (also called "rites"), have arisen, each claiming to provide the most accurate discovery of religious truth within the law. They include the *Hanafī* rite (with the largest number of adherents), the *Malīkī* rite, the *Shāfi'ī* rite, and the *Hanabalī* rite. The differences among these schools tend to rest upon matters of detail, rather than substantive belief. Nonetheless, they provide for a certain degree of contention within a system that seeks to eliminate that element. Beyond the *Sunni* heritage of Islam, the *Shī'ite* denomination offers a completely different approach to Islamic law, resting its authority upon the teachings of the caliphate, who have served as traditional sacred and secular leaders, descended from a different line that also can be traced to Mohammed.

Again, though, the belief that law is discovered, rather than "made," especially by judges, has distinguished a general heritage of Islamic law. Superficially, *Shari'a* appears to share, with the common law system, a deference for the legal opinions of previous jurists, while it seems to rely upon the authoritative writings of scholars that remains a prominent feature of the civil law system and tends to deny judges interpretive discretion. The search for analytical unity, though, reflects a persistent goal of the Western legal tradition in a broader sense. The process of analogy, and the need to reconcile the law with the needs and practices of the community (although the former consideration is expected to predominate), offers an interesting comparison with, and insight into, other aspects of the wider Western legal tradition, even within a secular context.

Comparing Western Religious and Secular Law

Western thought tends to divide all aspects of human existence into distinct categories. Therefore, religious law and secular law generally are treated as separate traditions that do not relate to each other. The belief that religion is tied to "otherworldly" considerations, rather than the "real world" of modern society, tends to intensify that perception. However, it is crucial to note that the rise of secular Western legal traditions, including legal positivism, have been incapable of occurring without an underlying focus upon fundamental beliefs and values. This foundation may not envision a particular ideal of God or the supernatural, but it does attempt to describe, and impose, a certain idea of legal "truth." The difference between Western religious and secular approaches do not appear to differ very much, when considered from that perspective.

Western secular law, especially under the positive law tradition, emphasizes structure and leaves content to the will of the sovereign. Western traditions of religious law may begin with a preconceived ideal of the sacred origins of law, but they translate it through a similar process. Legal content is left to God and religious authority, but the structure for expressing it remains consistent, even though it is inspired by the same theological considerations. The study of Western religion and law parallels, therefore, the development of Western law, generally. Therefore, its comparative study is useful, especially once the influence of these religious heritages upon current societies and their secular legal traditions are considered. Thus the study of Western religion and law advances this overall attempt to understand law, in its broadest sense.

References

John A. Abbo and Jerome D. Hannan, *The Sacred Canons: A Concise Presentation of the Current Disciplinary Norms of the Church*. St. Louis, Herder, 1957.

Charles Auerbach, *The Talmud: A Gateway to the Common Law*. Cleveland, Western Reserve University Press, 1952.

James A. Coriden, *An Introduction to Canon Law*. New York, Paulist, 2000.

Rodolphe A. J. De Seife, *The Shari'a: An Introduction to the Law of Islam*. San Francisco, Austin and Winfield, 1994.

James K. Gaynor, *Lawyers in Heaven*. Philadelphia, Dorrance, 1979.

Wael B. Hallaq, *Authority, Continuity, and Change in Islamic Law*. Cambridge, Cambridge University Press, 2001.

James Provost and Knut Walf, and Marcus Lefébure, eds. *Canon Law—Church Reality*. Edinburgh, T. and T. Clark, 1986.

John D. Rayner, *Jewish Religious Law: A Progressive Perspective*. New York, Berghahn, 1998.

Lawrence Rosen, *The Justice of Islam: Comparative Perspectives on Islamic Law and Society*. Oxford, Oxford University Press, 2000.

Moshe Silberg, *Talmudic Law and the Modern State*, Ben Zion Bokser, trans, Martin S. Wiener, ed. New York, Burning Book, 1973.

CHAPTER 8

Tribal Law

Conceptualizing the Tribe

The term "tribal" is broad and, potentially, ambiguous. It is not surprising, therefore, that a description of tribal *law* may be equally, or more, difficult to describe. However, it is important to engage in a brief exploration of this legal heritage. First, all humans are descended from peoples who were shaped by the precepts of tribal legal relationships and values. Second, it offers an even more stark contrast to the legal norms and values of both Eastern and Western modern traditions than these two variations provide to each other. Therefore, an understanding of tribal law from a comparative perspective, especially in terms of its pertinence toward a superior understanding of public law is, potentially, invaluable.

A tribe is not defined in ethnic or racial terms. That misunderstanding can be the basis for unfortunate acrimony and ignorant labeling. "Tribe" is a political, economic, and legal term, and it applies only to people who exist, currently, within a very particular category of active community. The vast majority of people of the twenty-first century do not live in a tribe, but are part of a *society*. Some people may claim a conscious adherence to both social and tribal associations. However, that identity is a matter of choice; it is not imposed from outside the community. This chapter will consider the legal relationships and values of people who consciously participate within the life of a tribe, in its most accurate and meaningful expression.

A tribe differs, for example, from an ethnic or racial group. A person may be regarded as descended from, and, thus, identified with, the Celtic ethnic group that commonly is traced to Europe. The Celts, as a whole, lived within tribal communities (according to tribal standards of social, political, and legal relationships) 2,000 years ago. However, it is incorrect to refer to a modern person of Celtic descent as being a member of a Celtic *tribe*. Tribal peoples, adhering to an understanding of tribal law, do, in fact, continue to exist, throughout the world, including some of the Beti of Africa, the Ainu of Japan, the Lakota of North America, the Guaraní of South America, the Polynesians of various Pacific islands, the Inuit of the Arctic regions, the Lapps of Scandinavia, the Aborigines of Australia, and many other peoples. It is the legal heritage of these communities, and similar communities that have preceded them, throughout history, that will be evaluated from a comparative perspective.

Patterns of Tribal Law

A single definition of tribal law does not exist. The diverse tribal communities of the world generally have not been influenced by each other, so they have not developed a strictly uniform system of law in the manner of conventional Eastern and Western traditions, nor in the institutional manner of the civil law and common law systems. However, a discernable concept of tribal law does exist; it has achieved a degree of similarity that is due to the very comparable political, social, and, especially, economic relationships that have arisen within all of these communities. So, while a strict definition or set of principles for tribal law does not emerge, basic legal themes can be revealed through an evaluation of these assorted tribal communities.

The first of these themes relates to a holistic approach that these communities tend to adopt toward their understanding of the world. Superficially, this theme seems to relate to a similar perspective found within Eastern culture. However, the tribal outlook derives from an economic imperative, in the broadest sense of the term. Tribal peoples are bound to the resources of the land they inhabit; their survival depends upon maintaining an often precarious environmental balance. Food, water, shelter, clothing, and all of the other necessities of existence are attained directly, through the coordinated efforts of the whole community. Prosperity also is dependent upon this relationship, which requires careful coordination of the community, as a whole, and a marshaling and maintenance of this symbiotic relationship. The people and their environment are one, and all other considerations stem from this imperative. This factor requires a particular type of organizing principle which, in turn, necessitates ordered relationships among members of the community.

An implicit legal relationship, in a pliant sense of the term, arises, almost spontaneously, from this "economic" necessity. The terms of that relationship appear to rely, generally, upon a concept of an implied consensus of the whole community. That consensus relies upon a peculiar division of responsibilities regarding those resources and the collective activities of the tribe. One of the most conspicuous features of that division of responsibilities is the fact that it is largely grounded upon family, and other kinship, ties.

The concept of kinship is central to the tribal legal order. Kinship groups normally include interrelated families, but the kinship bonds exist at different levels, from the immediate family to the clan. The tribe is regarded as the highest expression of kinship. Western terms such as "nation" also have been used as a rough translation for labeling this broad socio-political unit. The members, themselves, perceive their relationship to each other in exclusive terms. The name that members of a tribe often give themselves (a tendency that is especially common among the indigenous peoples of North America) frequently translates as "the people"—the sense being that they constitute, from their perspective, the world in whole and they are, collectively, the only "people" who matter to their own existence. All relationships within the tribe, especially from a "legal" perspective (as imposed by conventional Western standards) are grounded upon this sort of assumption, and positions of leadership generally are directed toward a coordination of this interdependent, mutually supportive, holistic existence.

Tribal Leadership

People who dominate a family, kinship group, or the tribe may appear, from an external perspective, to wield exclusive authority. Each level of kinship, from the head of an immediate family, to the leader of a kinship group, to an important figure exercising authority over the entire tribe, has its own leaders. These levels surround each member with increasingly broad circles of relationship, in which they remain part of each whole. The leaders of each unit exercise responsibility for coordinating the activities of their group with other groups and the larger whole. Therefore, their guidance often seems to be portrayed in absolute terms, although that external perception is somewhat misleading.

However, the role of the leader usually rests upon a foundation of consensus. Such persons may occupy a position, for example, because of some form of inheritance, and their authority may appear to be absolute, but they are tightly bound to expectations and responsibilities that are measured in terms of the prosperity of the people and their success in meeting the needs and expectations of other members of their group. Other members of this group, at all levels (family, kinship, tribe) are expected to be guided by these leaders, but a failure of a leader to wield that responsibility in a proper or beneficial manner can result in their admonition or, even, replacement.

Tribal Law and Property

This legal relationship of authority may be expressed best in terms of another basic legal relationship concerning the disposition of property. The conventional liberal democratic understanding of property does not apply to a true tribal legal context, for the idea of exclusive individual ownership is inconsistent with general tribal affiliations and values. However, a cursory observation of tribal norms might provide an impression that conventional attitudes toward property actually dominate this association, particularly in terms of the larger quantity of goods that appear to be possessed by various tribal leaders. That impression may suggest that persons with greater responsibility enjoy greater privileges regarding personal property. However, that external conclusion is somewhat simplistic.

This misconception may be due to a lack of distinction, on the part of observers, between property *ownership* and property *control*. Members of a tribe, including leaders, do not *own* property, in the conventional sense. However, they do *possess* it for the purpose of meeting their needs and the needs of other members of their family or group. Leaders play a pivotal role within that process. They control greater quantities of property, because their responsibilities are, correspondingly, greater. A tribal leader must have access to considerable stores of food and other forms of bounty, for example, because of expectations that the leader has a greater responsibility for providing for other tribal members through that largesse. This responsibility does, indeed, include greater privileges, including in terms of access to, and ability to use for one's own benefit, this relative wealth. But the understanding remains that this possession exists for a distributive purpose, also, and a tribal leader has an absolute obligation, in that respect, as do other leaders, including the head of a family in relation to other family members.

Shared tribal resources are controlled in a similar manner. Frequently, a particular asset of the entire tribe falls under the hereditary control of a particular kinship group. That control makes the resource more accessible to the members of the kinship group, and they derive advantages from that situation. Nonetheless, the kinship group is expected to control that resource for the benefit of all tribal members; a failure to conform to that expectation can result in a perceived violation of a legal obligation and subsequent consequences.

An example of this situation could involve a kinship group that controls a fertile fishing access. Members of this kinship group may determine the conditions of access for tribal members from other kinship groups, and they may maintain it in a manner that provides certain benefits to members of this kinship group. However, arbitrary denial of access to other members of the tribal community violates the expectations that accompany such a position. The kinship group leader may decide to regulate access because of scarcity, and that exercise of authority would be regarded as consistent with the needs of the tribe, even if it benefits members of the kinship group who are not, necessarily, so restricted.

The leader who decides that other groups will be denied access to this resource out of rivalry or spite also may have the authority to make that decision, so it may appear that this legal relationship is authoritarian in nature. But other tribal leaders (including those elders responsible for mediating such legal disputes) subsequently may determine that, while the kinship leader is within the permissible bounds of authority to commit such action on behalf of a single group, this decision is inconsistent with the broader needs of the tribe. So, it may be determined that this control of the fishing access should be taken from that kinship group and given, subsequently, to another kinship group that will control it in a manner that is beneficial to the whole community.

Tribal leaders may be chosen upon the basis of heredity, but certain positions also are filled upon the basis of apparent ability. Legal disputes may be submitted to leading members of the tribe who, because of their general experience and perceived wisdom and maturity, are respected for their abilities to render beneficial and just decisions. They often serve to retain a memory of the customs that have guided the community for several generations. The deference to customary law often is bolstered by a respect for ancestors who continue to be revered, as though they remain a part of the living community. The holistic perspective of many tribal peoples makes the Western concept of time an irrelevance, so custom is bolstered as a source of current legal norms. Customs generally are consistent, though, with the economic and social patterns of tribal existence, especially in terms of the relationship with the land and its resources. Therefore, custom serves to reinforce legal norms that arise, spontaneously, from the life of the community and its expectations.

Consensual Judgment and Decision Making

Although leaders may be required to act upon their own discretion over matters requiring immediate choices or in fulfillment of larger directives, the decisions relating to the welfare of the community and the overall policy it will follow generally is subject to the consensus of the whole. Tribes traditionally do not render such choices through Western democratic techniques, for a consensus differs substantially from the will of the majority. Therefore, for the purpose of providing direction to the community, the tribe often is divided into groups that reflect the broad positions and responsibilities of members, according to their capacities, experience, and talents. The preferences of each collective group then may be consolidated to reflect a consensus opinion of a kinship group or, even, a geographically distinct grouping, such as a village. These groups typically arrive at a consensus and, then, interact with other groups in order to achieve a broad consensus that will apply to the entire tribal association.

One example can be derived from the organization of the Iroquois Confederacy. This political coalition has united six different tribes, or nations, into a larger whole. Historically, each nation has consisted of a large number of villages, each one often corresponding to a kinship group and, in turn, consisting of a certain number of families. Furthermore, the tribe has been divided further into functional groups, such as the "young warriors," constituting vigorous youths who possess much spirit but lack experience and the maturity and wisdom it brings. Other such divisions include the mature warriors, the "mothers" (encompassing all adult women who nurture and care for the community), and the elders, whose age often precludes them from certain physical activities on behalf of the tribe but whose superior experience, maturity, and wisdom provide a critical perspective for the deliberations of the community. These groupings, together with family and kinship associations, have provided a basis for consensual policy making.

Each group, under this sort of arrangement, arrives at a consensus upon a policy, consistent with its own perspective and desires. Then, the groups confer with each other, often under the guidance of the elders and other leaders (including elders who play the role of judges concerning legal questions and disputes), until a broader consensus of some sort is achieved. The consensus of the village, as with each group, corresponds to a single will, even if certain individual members continue to object, privately. A meeting of all the villages results in a similar movement toward finding consensus, through deliberation, compromise, and a search for "common ground." This process can result in a consensus opinion for the nation, which, within the Iroquois example, would be brought to a council of the confederacy. The search for consensus among the nations may not succeed, in which case, each nation would be free to pursue its own policy, provided it does not harm the other members of the confederacy.

This example of the process of consensual policy making is indicative of the holistic theme that provides a firm basis for all political and legal relationships within a tribe. The mutual interdependence of the members of these communities, reinforced by ties of family and kinship and defined by roles, abilities, and responsibilities, exists in response to the needs of that community regarding their ultimate survival and prosperity. The economic relationship to the land and its resources is the key to this situation, and, since most human communities have altered this approach to their survival and prosperity, the presence of the tribe and its law have declined, globally.

The Significance of Tribal Legal Models

Nonetheless, tribal relations and tribal law offer a remarkable example of a lifestyle that continues to have an appeal, especially in terms of the collective identity and strong ties that can bind people together. It also offers an important contrast to modern legal traditions, especially among Western societies, that can provide a basis of evaluation that can illuminate the strengths and weaknesses of these contemporary norms. That process can be particularly useful in terms of comparative legal analysis, since tribal law is firmly directed toward an expression of the community, as a whole, rather than merely a vehicle for separate members to coexist and pursue their own desires.

Therefore, the tribal legal norms of the promotion of a holistic community, the distributive control of property for the benefit of that community, kinship ties and the leadership roles that emerge from it, collective divisions within the community, and the consensual approach to policy making and other decisions that affect the tribe are extremely useful to understand. Tribal law remains an important aspect of comparative law for scholars and, even, practitioners. That relevance is especially pertinent when trying to appreciate those current political systems that include, and continue to be influenced by, tribal communities.

References

Thomas Peter Ellis, *Welsh Tribal Law and Custom in the Middle Ages*. Aalen, Scientia Verlag, 1982.

Max Gluckman, *Politics, Law, and Ritual in Tribal Society*. Oxford, Blackwell, 1965.

Bradford W. Morse, ed., *Aboriginal Peoples and the Law*. Ottawa, Carleton University Press, 1989.

Alexander Nékám, *Experiences in African Customary Law*. Edinburgh, University of Edinburgh Centre of African Studies, 1966.

Frank Pommersheim, *Braid of Feathers: American Indian Law and Contemporary Tribal Life*. Berkeley, University of California Press, 1995.

K. S. Singh, ed., *Tribal Ethnography, Customary Law, and Change*. New Delhi, Concept, 1993.

CHAPTER 9

Unitary, Federal, and Confederal Systems

Single and Shared Sovereignty

Modern political and legal systems can be categorized according to the way they structure their expression of sovereign authority. Each state is defined as a sovereign unit (as explained within a previous chapter) in terms of the fact that it exercises political and legal power while it remains, simultaneously, free from any formal subordination (although it may succumb to informal external pressures in implementing its laws, especially as dictated by economic or military necessity) to any other political and legal power. However, that ultimate sovereignty does not necessarily reside within a single source. The structural choices available to a state have a profound effect upon its constitutional development and values. The position of sovereign authority within, and expressed through, that structure is even more significant. Therefore, it is critical to understand and appreciate the options available for affecting and recognizing this essential demonstration of supreme legal authority within a state.

The concept of a shared sovereignty does not undermine the position of the state, nor should it imply a lack of political and legal unity. This concept is distinct, though, from the merely structural organization of the state. A political and legal system can consist of varying levels and areas of authority, but ascertaining the final authority is key to determining its sovereign status. A system that is decentralized in its administration is not, necessarily, inconsistent with the presence of a centralized source of ultimate political authotity. Medieval feudal systems recognized the authority of noble authorities who ruled their lands with overwhelming dominion. Yet, the ultimate source of that authority still rested in a higher power, even if it proved to be, frequently, ineffective. A truly shared sovereign arrangement provides for an exclusive and enduring division of ultimate control that *remains* a permanent prerogative of these separate sources of authority, even if one of them asserts an overarching role of providing for the international personality of the state, particularly in terms of maintaining a fundamental constitutional identity.

Unitary Government

A state that expresses a single source of sovereign authority is defined as having a unitary system of government. Unitary governments provided the genesis for the modern expression of the idea of sovereignty, and they continue to predominate, globally. They offer a relatively simple means for depicting this political and legal authority and advancing the legitimacy of that sovereign claim. The development of unitary government also offers insights into the motives and influences that have shaped modern constitutionalism.

The most important purpose for establishing unitary government has been, arguably, the promotion of the rule of law and the broad establishment of the principles of legal positivism. A single, unified source of legal sovereignty reinforces the belief that these consistent, recognizable principles are immutable. The legal supremacy thus established advances the cause of nationalism, particularly through the framing of a consolidated nation-state. The articulation of that national identity, and the advancement of the social, cultural, economic, and political priorities of the nation, can find an unambiguous enunciation through the enforcement of this single, sovereign will.

Countries that have sought to subsume competing regional and group identities in order to achieve a stable political system appear to have preferred the imposition of a unitary system of government. A country such as Great Britain offers a good example of this sort of unitary state. It includes the strong, geographically and culturally visible nations of England, Scotland, and Wales. Well-structured and effective levels of government exist at the regional, county, local, and, now, national levels. However, these governments ultimately are undermined as potential sources of political rebellion, because sovereign authority remains vested in only one source of British government, with the Parliament at Westminster. Therefore, regional or county governments, for example, that threaten the unity of the state can be (and have been) simply eliminated by the central government. This unitary advantage may not be successful in quelling continued discontent or addressing the underlying forces (including nationalist identification) that motivate these problems. However, with time, the unitary authority established through the union of Great Britain and the acceptance of a unitary system has advanced a certain stability that might have proven to be impossible had another level of government possessed real sovereign, in addition to delegated, political and legal power.

Unitary systems of government can be effective in promoting this sort of sovereign legitimacy and stability. However, they also can be extremely ineffective in responding to strong national sentiments and desires for political goals among the peoples that comprise a diverse society. These strengths and limitations are more readily considered through a comparison of the unitary model with its alternatives, particularly the federal system of government.

Federal Government

The emergence of federal arrangements of sovereign authority has been relatively a more recent legal development. Generally, a federal system is the result of a certain number of fully sovereign, or potentially sovereign, political states uniting for the purpose of promoting their common advantage. The motivating factors often are economic and military, and it stems from a recognition, among these states, of a mutual advantage or necessity. National identity generally does not prompt the creation of a federal system, but a successful federal system often can provide the basis for the emergence of a sense of nationalism among the peoples of the various states that comprise this system of shared sovereignty. This possibility is revealed through the example of the world's most prominent federal system, the United States.

Federal systems conventionally are formed when several sovereign states agree to surrender a portion of their sovereignty and delegate it to a central government that will exercise that delegated authority over all of them. This description requires an ability to overcome an apparent conceptual contradiction; since the definition of a sovereign asserts that it is not subject to any other political or legal authority, this surrender of sovereign authority should be, theoretically, untenable. However, a federal arrangement mandates that those areas of responsibility that are retained by the separate states remain their *exclusive* realm of authority, which may not be transgressed, under any circumstance, unless they consent to a renegotiation of this sovereign relationship.

The sovereign authority that is delegated to the central government include those powers necessary for a state to function at the international level, where ultimate sovereign identity is recognized. Foreign relations, international commerce, and military and naval affairs are the most consistent of these powers. Meanwhile, the sovereign authority retained by the component states frequently include those powers that pertain to the maintenance of internal order, social services, and relationships among members of society. This sort of arrangement also can (and, frequently, does) exist within a unitary system; the difference, again, lies within the fact that the sharing of power is sovereign, in nature, and cannot be altered or denied, including by the "higher" level of political and legal authority.

Federal systems are established from a desire to promote a mutual self-interest among the states that join it. They often find themselves vulnerable, in some fashion, especially in terms of a need for permanent economic cooperation or an ability to defend themselves against actual and potential aggressors. Another motive can be derived from an adaptation of the liberal democratic emphasis upon limited government. The division of sovereign authority among different levels of government can be compared to the assumptions inherent in the separation of powers within a single government. The division of the expression of sovereign power theoretically makes it increasingly difficult for government officials to abuse that delegated power, since they find themselves in political competition with other representatives of sovereign power. A term that has been applied to a federal arrangement is a "social compact." Arguably, it reflects this sentiment by imitating the philosophical concept of a "social contract" that has been used to describe and justify liberal democratic conceptualizations of retained rights and popular sources of sovereignty, although a federal system can exist within a non-liberal society.

This reference to social contract theory and its potential effect upon government power is reinforced by the relationship that tends to emerge among these sovereign "partners." Competition arises, within federal systems, concerning the extent of sovereign power exercised by each level of government. The result of the original agreement to share sovereign authority and the subsequent implementation of that arrangement generally fails to resolve the extent of this relationship. Governments at each level tend to seek ways to aggrandize their authority, necessarily at the expense of the other levels of sovereign government.

When the component states succeed in this goal, the result is a trend toward a decentralization of sovereign authority, and when the central government prevails in this struggle, the result is a centralizing trend. Different federal systems experience different degrees of centralization or decentralization, resulting in policies and practices that reflect this struggle and its consequences, especially for the members of society. That struggle has profound consequences for the development of the values, interpretation, and actually functioning of constitutional traditions which will be evaluated within the chapters devoted to these countries.

A federal system can be described as a "community of communities," allowing for varying societies to merge into a shared identity. The American political motto *e pluribus unum* ("from many, one") reflects that ideal. But one consequence of achieving a federal system is the expectation of the permanence of that sovereign arrangement. Another variation upon this theme addresses that consideration.

Confederal Government

The term "confederal" sometimes seems to suggest, to many observers, merely a more decentralized sovereign arrangement than a federal system offers. However, a true confederacy is not just a more decentralized version of federalism, nor is it a simple synonym for the term "federalism." True confederal systems are relatively rare within the modern world, but recent trends in international relations may make this sort of sovereign arrangement increasingly relevant, especially for the political processes of the twenty-first century and the ongoing evolution of constitutional law, throughout the world.

Considerable similarities do, indeed, exist between federal and confederal systems. Indeed, the similarities appear to outweigh their differences, overwhelmingly. They both tend to result from the union of fully sovereign states in pursuit of mutual advantage, protection, or other forms of self-interest. They both delegate sovereign authority from these states to a central government created as a result of that process. Competition often arises within both of them concerning the degree of sovereign authority actually held and exercised by each level of government. They often are not prompted by a sense of national identity, but they both can help to forge such an identity. They both can be extremely significant sources for the emergence and development of a distinct and enduring constitutional tradition.

But confederal systems differ from federal systems in one, extremely significant way. The states that comprise a confederal system retain the ultimate prerogative to reclaim their delegated sovereign authority and abandon this relationship in favor of establishing their own, fully expressed sovereign presence as a member of the international community. Therefore, it is possible to characterize these states as providing merely a conditional delegation of their sovereign prerogatives, rather than an absolute surrender of that ultimate political power.

Switzerland offers a prime example of a confederal system, with its cantons that joined together to create a union with a central government. Originally, the sovereign ties of the cantons to the central government were extremely loose; even now, they retain a degree of sovereign control over many of their affairs that suggests this dominant position of the cantons. The Confederate States of America were established as a confederal alternative to the United States, particularly in terms of the premise of "states' rights" and the insistence upon a "right of seccession" for all states, which the American government vigorously resisted. The Union victory, during the American Civil War, reimposed a federal system upon the defeated Confederates, including the principle that the sovereign authority of these states could *not* include the capacity to withdraw from that union and reclaim its full sovereign authority.

A more contemporary example of a confederal system is the international organization in which sovereign countries agree to surrender certain limited control over aspects of their social, economic, defense, and legal policies and institutions. The most conspicuous example of this arrangement is the European Union. Arguably, it can be labeled a confederal system, because its members do surrender sovereign authority over certain key areas (including economic regulation, military forces, aspects of commercial law, and human rights), while retaining the option of reclaiming all of their sovereign authority and departing the organization. Like the Swiss cantons, practical considerations make that sort of reclaiming of sovereignty unlikely. However, the fact that the option is available, and the sovereign authority is delegated from independent states to some form of central authority, does conform to this description of confederal government and, therefore, offers a potentially important role for this option during the twenty-first century.

The Constitutional Significance of Divided Sovereign Power

The seeming resurgence of nationalism, during the late twentieth and early twenty-first centuries, has posed severe problems for global stability. Demands for self-determination can result in the disintegration of states and their replacement with potentially unstable political entities, particularly since this desire for sovereign identity often assumes that it can be achieved only through the creation of a completely sovereign unitary system. Federalism, in particular, has offered an alternative solution to this dilemma.

Constitutional government can exist at a central or sub-federal level. American states, for example, have their own constitutions, in addition to the United States Constitution. These constitutions can be framed for these emerging nations to provide sovereign authority over those features that provide the most essential expression of that national identity, while maintaining another, central level of sovereign authority to address other legitimate responsibilities of a modern country, especially in areas of international relations and security. Meanwhile, it is crucial to recognize and appreciate these systemic alternatives of sovereign authority, for they play a crucial, and often underappreciated, function, in the shaping of a constitutional tradition.

References

Daniel J. Elazar, Constitutionalizing Globalization: *The Postmodern Revival of Confederal Arrangements*. Lanham, MA, Rowman and Littlefield, 1998.
Daniel J. Elazar, *Exploring Federalism*. London, University of Alabama Press, 1987.
Murray Forsythe, ed., *Federalism and Nationalism*. Leicester, University of Leicester Press, 1989.
Carl J. Friedrich, *Trends of Federalism in Theory and Practice*. London, Pall Mall, 1968.
Preston T. King, *Federalism and Federation*. Baltimore, Johns Hopkins University Press, 1982.
Frederick K. Lister, *The European Union, the United Nations, and the Revival of Confederal Governance*. Westport, CT, Greenwood, 1996.
Edward C. Page and Michael J. Goldsmith, eds., *Central and Local Government Relations: A Comparative Analysis of West European Unitary States*. London, Sage, 1987.
Bertus de Villiers, ed., *Evaluating Federal Systems*. Cape Town, Juta, 1994.

CHAPTER 10

Crime, Injury, Punishment, and the State

The Rule of Law

A familiar ideal of modern legality has been the commonly repeated phrase "the rule of law, not of men." The phrase may be somewhat archaic (referring to, as it suggests, monarchical or oligarchical governance, particularly from a male perspective), but its sentiment remains pertinent. Sovereign authority has come to express itself, within the modern world, through positive law. That legal expression advances the agenda of a sovereign authority but it also, ironically, imposes a self-limitation upon that same sovereign government. The rule of law binds the sovereign, as much as it binds its subjects.

One of the most important purposes of the rule of law is the elimination of arbitrary and unpredictable legal behavior. Theoretically, of course, the sovereign cannot be compelled to adopt any particular form of legal behavior but is free to behave with complete discretion, in this respect. But the absence of such restraint could be, arguably, so chaotic that a meaningful expression of sovereign will would prove to be impossible. As a general principle, the rule of law simply refers to the ideal that no person, institutions, or source of authority within society is "above the law." The sovereign establishes, through the institutions of the state, legal prescriptions and, then, commits itself to follow them. Since these legal rules would be extremely difficult to discern without the benefit of an underlying rationale (logically expounded through a consistent legal system and its institutions) the need for an overarching constitutional tradition to define and guide that law becomes an increasingly apparent necessity.

The concept of the rule of law is fairly simple. Its underlying premise is advanced further by the ideological assumptions of liberal democracy, especially in terms of the priority of limited government. However, it rests upon certain other concepts and institutions that need to be defined and clarified, also. The concept of the "state," both as an expression of sovereign authority, a description of government, and an institutional political and legal abstraction, needs to be explored. Further, the roleof that state in upholding and enforcing this "rule of law" also needs to be considered. Finally, the way this concept frames other legal roles and responsibilities of the state, especially in terms of regulating private lives within a public context, is a subject that should be examined, especially in terms of its ability to illuminate this somewhat abstruse, though very basic, concept of the "rule of law."

The State as a Legal Concept

The most readily accepted purpose of a government, especially within a liberal democratic society, is the protection of that society and its members. Arguably, the most important area of public law for a government is criminal law. However, it is not the only legal responsibility of the state, and it is extremely important to understand this matter, particularly since it is the overall legal system of a country that defines and legitimizes these legal responsibilities and the power necessary to accomplish it. Therefore, these concepts need to be identified and defined.

The state, as a term describing the source of practical political power within a political system (or, also, used as a slightly simplistic synonym for "government"), is, essentially, a legal concept. The description and parameters of its authority depend upon the way its relationship to sovereign authority is understood within its respective system. That understanding consequently affects the interpretation and application of all aspects of public law, particularly, but not exclusively, in relation to this role as the legitimate defender of society, its interests, and its members. That conception is particularly pertinent to a liberal democratic definition of the state, which dominates most of the world's legal systems. But it is even more widely pertinent.

Three optional perceptions of the state merit particular attention. The first perception is the state as an unlimited patriarch, which can be associated (though not, necessarily, exclusively) with classic conservative thought. It also can be related to the idea of the transitional socialist state described by Marxist (particularly Leninist) political theorists. Thomas Hobbes, the classic conservative political theorist, insisted that a proper "social contract" between sovereign and subjects really is a form of submission from the latter group to the former ruler. Limits must not be imposed upon the sovereign; otherwise, chaos will result, since people naturally are selfish, wanton, violent, and, even, stupid. The strong sovereign is the only hope for maintaining the order and stability necessary for a stable and prosperous society.

This image of the state represents law as a tool that promotes the will of the sovereign. It is as applicable to the sovereign democratic majority as it is to the sovereign monarch, and it should be unchallenged, or it will fail to be effective. The need to protect society is the overriding justification for this depiction of the state, and law, from this perspective, enforces the will of society, maintains order, and is not a constraint upon the sovereign but a tool of the government as its agent.

The liberal democratic image of the state stresses the notion that law provides a self-imposed limit upon the state. The concept of the rule of law is an expression of that belief. The state remains an instrument of the sovereign will, but it is a restrained agent, protecting the fundamental values of liberty and individualism that are not necessarily consistent with the sovereign will of an electoral plurality or majority. The concept of a rule of law relays that perspective by providing a sense of self-constraint, compelling the government to interact with society according to a commonly applicable set of regulations and legal principles.

Another way of perceiving the legal role of the state is in terms of the government as a mediator for society. This image is an excellent expression of the ideal of the state as a "neutral arbiter." Communitarian visions of liberal democracy tend to favor this image, even while acknowledging the legitimacy of the protective and coercive role a government assumes for the benefit of a sovereign people. The concept of the government as a mediator tends to emphasize the principle of human freedom, reducing the state to a "public servant" in as literal a sense as possible.

This image conceives of society as a legal "stage," maintained by the state, where members of that society compete. The mediation role of government makes it both a referee and a cipher for a democratic sovereign. But the assumption of state neutrality depends upon a willingness to believe that a government is unwilling to use this power for ends that may differ from the sovereign will. The notion of government obedience to the sovereign ignores the enormity of the power that has been delegated and the human tendency to wield that power.

Some critics, therefore, would regard as naive the image of the state as a willingly neutral arbiter, or mediator, for society. Other critics might entertain a similar attitude toward the image of the state as bound by the will of the sovereign—a force that would wield power, independently, but for the strictly limited description of the scope of its power, as imposed by the "social contract." Additional critics might regard as cynical the image of the state as an unlimited patriarch or, at least, treat it as failing to acknowledge the very real constraints that a society (particularly a liberal democratic one) imposes upon any government. But this liberal democratic image of the limited state increasingly has become, at least theoretically, the most persuasive description, especially in terms of its role as law maker, law enforcer, and law interpreter. Therefore, many assumptions of comparative law are grounded upon that liberal democratic image of the state.

Categorizing the Law

The efforts of legal positivists to impose a rational, and empirically sustainable, order upon the law has resulted in a classification of laws according to their purposes, scope, and characteristics. The most basic division is between "public" and "private" law. The difference between these two categories is based upon the relationship that they impose between the state and the subjects who are governed. Furthermore, this distinction is bound to the larger separation of public and private realms, with the former area of society being defined by the fact that it includes those matters that are, properly, the responsibility of the state, especially in terms of its responsibility for protecting society.

This categorization has become so useful that it even is applied to international law. This process has become part of the "science" of law advanced with great effectiveness by legal positivists in the tradition of John Austin. But it also has been a concern of other legal scholars, and it is an additional product of the rational emphasis of humanism, the Age of Reason, and the general development of the modern period, especially among Western cultures. Therefore, an introductory explanation of this categorization is useful for appreciating certain influences upon the development of public law, particularly in terms of its structural cultivation.

Public Law

That role is defined particularly effectively by liberal theory. John Locke argued that the only power that people, living in a "state of nature," have delegated to government, through the "social contract," is the "right of self-defense." But an even better explanation of the role of the liberal state was provided by John Stuart Mill, the nineteenth-century philosopher, statesman, and son of James Mill, the foundational utilitarian philosopher. John Stuart Mill strongly argued that the only legitimate purpose of a government (echoing the liberal presumptions of Locke and other theorists) is the protection of society from "harm." Certain threats obviously fall under this label of "harm," such as military invasion, internal violence, or other direct threats to the life, safety, and property of the members of society. But this term is malleable, for "harm" can be ascribed to actions that pollute the environment, undermine the economy, leave people financially destitute, or destroy a society's sense of well-being. Liberal democratic societies continue to grapple with this definition of "harm," especially in terms of policy formulation and the extension of government powers. It can be expanded into a complex concept, but its basic parameters can be employed for the purpose of identifying that legal area falling under the government's most immediate responsibility for protecting and regulating society, which can be defined, broadly, as public law.

The supreme expression of public law is found within a constitution. Indeed, as previously noted, constitutions define the political system and all other areas of law for a society. Constitutional law performs a vital institutional role by establishing the means for creating, enforcing, and interpreting law. It also describes the legitimate powers of government, the areas in which public policy may be made, the basic values the society embraces, and the limits of the law.

Under the umbrella of constitutional law, other categories of public law emerge. Administrative law often is the most underappreciated category, since it can appear to be very mundane to the casual observer. But its responsibility for enacting the bureaucratic and regulatory consequences of government power and the policies it produces makes it not only indispensable but, also, the most pervasive category of law. Administrative law makes possible the fulfillment of those laws that sanction public policy. It can take the form of policy statutes made by a legislature, decrees made by executive authority, or the regulations authorized by these decrees and statutes and promulgated by civil servants, on behalf of the sovereign and in accordance with its broad wishes, even if the civil servants are granted wide discretion over this legal process of implementation and enforcement. The vast majority of the legal rules, standards, and other requirements of a modern society are derived from administrative law. It is a testament to the complexities of modern industrial and post-industrial societies, the expansive nature of the modern state (including liberal, socialist, and conservative versions), especially in terms of daily life, the ideological justifications that have evolved in support of this expansion, and the expectations of modern people regarding the bureaucratic role of the state and the legal means for fulfilling those expectations.

The effect of business, trade, and industry upon the public good results in another category of public law known, generically, as commercial law. Much of this legal area overlaps administrative law, since much of the related activity is regulatory in nature. Nonetheless, a distinct category of commercial law provides the general rules that govern all economic transactions. It emerged, historically, as a body of law distinct from the political development of legal norms and practices, governed by the independent guilds, in cooperation with each other.

Commercial law plays an important role in establishing legal norms and standards for international commerce, in addition to domestic economic activity. Concepts of commercial fairness, honesty, standards of quality, and principles guiding transactions are included within its scope, in addition to the administrative consequences of this legal expression. Economic imperatives of modern legal systems make commercial law a crucial component of the public realm.

Most casual observers, though, might conceive of criminal law as the ultimate expression of the public role of the state. Criminal law fulfills two basic purposes for modern societies: It compels obedience to the state; it protects society from direct harm. The definition of that harm need not be restricted to physical violence. Any action or condition can be "criminalized," provided that the state can, on behalf of the sovereign, offer a justification for perceiving it as harmful and, thus, in the interest of society to oppose. This justification fits a liberal definition of the state particularly well, but it is a rationale that also is pertinent to other ideological and philosophical conceptions of law. In fact, it is this role of government that becomes most effectively labeled as the general "police powers" of the state, and it often is perceived as the most appropriate purpose of most, if not all, conceptions of the state, especially through that enforcement arm that is, indeed, generically identified as the "police."

All ideological systems acknowledge the legitimacy of the state's enforcement of a criminal law. They differ, though, in the precise definitions of those actions or conditions that constitute a legitimate threat to society and, thus, a "crime." A person who steals from another person typically violates the criminal law. However, it also is possible to claim that a person who pollutes the environment, commits a forgery, undermines the prevailing economic system, challenges the authority of the government, frightens other people, or, even, offends a popular concept of moral behavior may violate the criminal law of a particular society. The key to this refinement lies within the constitutional norms that provide the state a means for arriving at its particular interpretation of "harm," as expressive of the elemental beliefs and values of the sovereign.

But another common effect of the criminal law is the way it classifies the relationship between the state and its "subjects," defined as the legal "persons" who operate under, and are constrained by, the rule of law. Again, though, this relationship is refined according to the negative standards that the state identifies as "criminal," in addition to the positive actions the state is expected to take on behalf of these subjects. Although the legal activities of the state are most frequently expressed through administrative law, it is not surprising that the more dramatic, comforting, and potentially threatening role of government that the criminal law represents tends to preoccupy the attention of the typical observer, enhancing this emphasis upon criminal law as an especially conspicuous expression of public law.

Private Law

Private law is more conventionally labeled "civil law." That term is descriptive of the role it plays in mediating relationships among citizens, in particular, and civil society, in general. The term "private" law may provide, though, a less confusing label, since the term "civil law" can be confused with the institutional system of the same name that exists, in one or another form, as the institutional expression of law within a majority of the world's countries. However, the term "private" also can be confusing, since it also is used to describe that realm that should fall outside the scope of the state, especially from a liberal perspective. The phrases "private law" and "civil law" often are used interchangeably; likewise, both nomenclatures may be used within this chapter.

This category of civil, or private, law invokes the role of the state as a mediator for members of society. Its most essential purpose is the prevention of the disruptive effect of private quarrels, or the tendency of people to "take the law into their own hands." Ancient civilizations, such as the Athenian city-state, made this consideration a central justification for the imposition of law by the state. Civil law establishes norms that guide personal behavior. It reconciles disputes that inevitably arise when the interests of private people come into conflict with each other. The absence of any such conflict results in the activity or condition remaining entirely private and, thus, beyond the normal concern of the state.

One important category of civil law is designated as "family law." It advances the interest of the state in the perpetuation and regulation of personal relationships. It often focuses upon the welfare of children, the role of parenting, and the regulation of the marriage contract, including its dissolution. Patriarchal governments often find a particular interest in this category of law, but even liberal societies feel the need to authorize legal control over these very personal matters.

Generally, civil law, as a broad category, is responsible for mediating private disputes that incur a public implication. This sovereign responsibility includes the weighing of evidence, considerations of the public welfare, the assessment of appropriate compensation and penalties, and the promotion of social fairness. The most frequent civil disputes involve conflicting claims over property and charges that one party has injured another party. This conflict generally is expressed through the process of parties "suing" each other, although the precise procedure followed varies, according to the legal system in use and differing constitutional values. Still, the general role of the state remains the same; indeed, the government, itself, may become a party to a civil suit, in its capacity as a subject of the same rule of law.

Individual disputants pursue civil cases of "personal action." Controversies affecting large numbers of people (such as an industry that allegedly harms all of its customers with a faulty product) can be presented as "class action" suits. Civil law cases are not necessarily confined to a single sort of direct conflict, even within a common law system. Nonetheless, the general principle inherent within a category of private, or civil, law remains relatively consistent. The state exercises ultimate legal authority on behalf of the sovereign, even within personal disputes. The government generally has no immediate stake in their outcome, except for maintaining order and stability within society by barring the private settlement of such disputes. Civil law differs from public law because it is not tied to the direct fulfillment of a government imperative to protect society from a particular harm or to formulate and enforce a specific public policy. Yet both categories conform to general legal principles enshrined within the heritage of its legal system and the express directives and fundamental values of its constitutional tradition.

Penology

The enforcement of the law requires, in the last resort, recourse to penal law, which is another category of public law. The justification for the state's authority to punish is, essentially, the same as its general legal legitimacy, as previously described. Furthermore, most ideological defenses of the role of the state, including liberal democracy, contend that the state, by its political nature, not only may employ constrained violence in support of its responsibilities, but it has a monopoly over that sanctioned violence.

Only the government may raise armed forces (unless it specifically authorizes the presence and use of private armed units), vigilante actions generally are prohibited, and retribution, even concerning private conflicts, normally is reserved to the government, alone. Exceptions to this principle exist (such as the necessity of defending oneself against an immediate threat of physical violence, in the absence of government police forces), but it offers an important insight into the exclusive government power to punish.

Penology, as an area of study and as a basis for establishing penal policy, stresses a variety of motivations and rationales for the different options available for punishment. Liberal societies often stress the primary responsibility of a government to protect society from harm. A person who has committed a crime poses a demonstrable threat to the members of society, and a particular penalty, such as incarceration, can serve to remove that threat. Utilitarian legal reformers (whose ideas were expounded within a previous chapter) offered important insights into the strategy of punishment as deterrence. However, they also argued that, since punishment is a form of "pain," which should not be unnecessarily imposed, its use must be restricted to the minimal degree needed to alleviate the "pain" of a particular crime and, thus, promote the "pleasure" of society. Thus punishment intended as deterrence should be proportionally imposed, with lighter sentences for lesser crimes and harsher penalties for more serious crimes.

Liberal democratic societies often have tended to perceive punishment as compensation for an abstract "loss" incurred by society as a result of an offense. The concept of "paying a debt to society" is derived from this proprietary conceptualization of crime as a "taking" and punishment as being restorative, especially in terms of restoring intangible, collective "property," such as an emotional sense of security, lost life, and destroyed goods. Social and philosophical reformers of the nineteenth and twentieth centuries, particularly a school of thought known as the "pragmatists" (who sought to measure the value of policies according to their success in achieving practical results for society), stressed a belief that punishment also should serve to rehabilitate criminal offenders, so they can be reintegrated into society as useful and contributing members.

However, many legal systems have experienced another, more basic motivation for punishment. The fear prompted by transgressors of law, and the anger of sovereigns against any such challenge to their authority, have promoted "revenge" as a strong motivating factor in the development of penal law, throughout human history. Penal law has become an expression of fear and anger. The fact that the state has had a legitimate interest in preventing private acts of retaliation as injurious to general stability and security has shifted this motive from victims to government. It is, arguably, the only plausible reason for the persistence of execution as a form of punishment, particularly within a liberal democratic society, although almost all modern democracies have abolished this "capital," or highest expression, of punishment.

Regardless of specific motives or means of implementation, penal law is a prime, and necessary, example of the state's use of public law as an expression of sovereign will and a tool of its own authority. It forms a very conspicuous part of modern legal systems, with many civil law systems reserving large sections of their civil codes to its promulgation. Penology offers a critical analysis of this pivotal legal and public policy category, especially for the legal comparativist who seeks to gain greater insights into the basic workings and underlying rationales of various legal systems and, especially, constitutional traditions.

Tort

Civil disputes often are responses to some sort of injury. The Norman French word for a "wrong" (especially in the sense of such an injury) is *tort*. Like many such terms (Norman French became, like Middle English, a source of a medieval legal lexicon that has contributed to the modern evolution of law), the concept of a tort has become an integral part of most legal systems. Tortious penalties offer a counterpart to the criminal sanctions of the penal law, so it is useful to gain an introductory understanding of this concept in support of broader comparative analysis of between public and private realms of law.

The sort of loss that occurs through an injury very seldom can be redeemed, directly. Therefore, the state bears the responsibility for determining, and enforcing, an equivalent remedy of compensation. Furthermore, the state's responsibility for mediating private disputes includes an interest in deterring future disputes, restoring public confidence in the basic fairness of economic and social activities, and promoting a general public good. Therefore, the remedy sanctioned by government within civil disputes frequently does not merely seek to compensate, but also attempts to impose additional penalties that will advance this larger purpose.

This mechanism can be complicated. The process of "converting" an injury, as demonstrated through the legal system, requires an ability to translate different measures of value. The liberal principle of "property" offers a good basis for this abstract reasoning, since anything that can be exchanged within a marketplace, under a liberal regime, qualifies as "property" that can be converted from one form (such as an injured body part) to another form (such as money) for purposes of fulfilling this judicial role. Ascribing a specific value to other factors involved in a tort, such as liability for negligence and compensation for "potential" future lost property (such as a lucrative career in sports that is ended through an accident) also necessitates careful deliberation and places an additional burden upon the state.

Tort law is immense and complex. However, the feature of compensation can be understood, particularly at a theoretical level, within this extremely brief format. An appreciation of this guiding principle, even briefly, provides a basis for future comparative considerations of legal norms and values, especially when they are publicly expressed.

Law and the State

All ideas require some sort of medium in order to be conveyed to humans. Law is no exception. While ideas can be conveyed as theoretical abstractions, they can be practically realized only through some tangible source of expression. The state, which is, itself, a theoretical abstraction, provides that medium of legal expression.

However, the state is only a legal vessel. It does not generate the ideas that it relays. The sovereign that sanctions and initiates the state (including the more specific institutional concept of a government) is needed for that purpose. Meanwhile, within the modern world, the sovereign generally lacks the ability to convey these fundamental beliefs and values, directly, especially when that sovereign is a relatively intangible democratic community. Therefore, a constitution is needed.

Constitutional law is the ultimate source of all other legal norms and values for a society. It describes the necessary philosophical foundation, creates the mediating political institutions, justifies the practical functions of the state, and provides the legal unity and consistency for all other categories of law that emerge from it. The comparative study of law cannot be meaningfully approached without recourse to this constitutional element, nor can constitutions be understood and compared without an assessment of this functional aspect of law and the state.

References

Thomas J. Biersteker and Cynthia Weber, eds., *State Sovereignty as Social Construct.* Cambridge, Cambridge University Press, 1996.

Daniel Engster, *Divine Sovereignty: The Origins of Modern State Power.* DeKalb, IL, Northern Illinois University Press, 2001.

George P. Fletcher, *Rethinking Criminal Law.* Oxford, Oxford University Press, 2000.

H. L. A. Hart, *Punishment and Responsibility: Essays in the Philosophy of Law.* Oxford, Clarendon, 1995.

Margaret C. Jasper, *The Law of Personal Injury.* Dobbs Ferry, NY, Oceana, 2000.

Leo Katz, Michael S. Moore, Stephen J. Morse, eds., *Foundations of Criminal Law.* New York, Foundation, 1999.

Peter Lewisch, *Punishment, Public Law Enforcement, and the Protective State.* Vienna, Springer-Verlag, 1995.

Marshall S. Shapo, *Basic Principles of Tort Law.* St. Paul, West, 1999.

CHAPTER 11

Property and Contract

Arguably, the most basic of all legal institutions, throughout history, has been the contract. The rise of liberal ideology has refined the modern understanding of contracts through its articulation of the principle of "property" in a strong, and highly influential, way. It has become a central focus of much modern legal education and training. Therefore, a comparative analysis of contracts necessitates, from a modern perspective, an additional analysis of the way that property is expressed as a distinctly legal institution. These features of law are so fundamental to modern legal interpretations that broader legal studies can be undermined without a prerequisite introduction to them—even if it is extremely cursory.

Property

The theoretical definition of property advanced by liberal ideology has shaped the modern understanding of that legal concept, even within non-liberal societies. Two categories of property exist for expressing this theoretical ideal. One of these categories reflects a traditional conception of tangible property that was particularly pertinent to the medieval origins of the Western legal tradition. The other broad category reflects the abstract understanding of property as refined by modern liberal political and legal theorists.

The first definitional category is "real property." The term *real* does not refer to the tangible nature of this category of property (as the English word "real" suggests), but to the Spanish origin of the word *real*, or "royal." Medieval legal theories of property emphasized the fact that the economy was grounded upon the land and its possession. It also promoted the belief that all land, within a kingdom, belonged to the royal sovereign (who could distribute its exclusive use to subjects throughout the realm), even if practical control actually rested with local aristocrats. Nonetheless, this overwhelming importance of landed property was responsible for the permanent and prominent place of real property as a legal concept. Even after the collapse of the feudal system, land, and all tangible property associated with it, retains this sense of traditional prominence.

Classifications of Property

Real property is contrasted with "personal" property. All attributes of a person's personality that can be converted from one commodity to another can be regarded as personal property. That property can exist in a tangible form, such as money, goods, or other physical assets, or it can exist in an intangible form, such as labor, intellect, and talent. It is conventional to refer to property in terms of measurable "assets." Some tangible property additionally can be regarded in terms of "liquid" assets (the imagery refers to the conception that this sort of property can "flow," easily) that exist as a unit of exchange that can be readily used for purchasing other property.

Some intangible property additionally can be regarded in terms of "potential" assets. The value of this property is anticipated, much like the proverbial eggs that are not valued by themselves but for their future status as chickens, after they have hatched and the subsequently produced chicks have grown to maturity. A person's talent, such as a musician or athlete, is treated in the same way, since its value is not realized until these talented persons have exchanged the use of their talent for monetary compensation.

The importance of the concept of potential assets is revealed in tort cases, when the value of an injury to a talented person is not measured in terms of the current damage but in terms of the value that person's talents *would* have produced, had they been sufficiently healthy. In a sense, the defendant in a legal tort action is accused of indirectly depriving the injured person of any potential property, in addition to any tangible loss to personal body or goods that may have been incurred, immediately. It is particularly important to appreciate this abstract conception of property, for it helps to explain certain aspects of the modern concept of a contract *and* it is usefulness for interpreting some of the underlying assumptions expressed within liberal democratic legal traditions. It also provides an excellent illustration of an application of the abstract liberal principle of "property" to an actual society and its legal system.

In fact, property has become so central to most legal systems *because* of the dominance of liberal democratic legal norms and values, even within non-democratic societies. However, the concept, and its importance, clearly precedes the rise of the modern period, with all civilizations, throughout the world, placing particular emphasis upon this theme throughout history. The concept of a contract is just as ancient and widespread, and its evaluation is equally important for gaining a meaningful appreciation of comparative perspectives of modern law.

Contract

Traditionally, an agreement between two parties, especially including some sort of permanent exchange, constitutes a "contract." This concept also has been used to describe more abstract relationships, involving more diverse numbers of participants, such as a legacy shared among generations, a covenant between people and a deity, a common bond that unites a people and their purposes, and the ideological construct of a "social contract" among people, between subjects and sovereign, or between a sovereign people and their delegated representatives in government.

Modern contract law, particularly as a product of commercial law, is highly technical, vast, and complex. Law students typically devote a very large portion of their professional education to the study of contract law. However, this challenging endeavor generally constitutes an examination and memorization of multitudinous variations upon a few, relatively simple themes. A cursory introduction to these elemental themes will not provide a professionally meaningful understanding of contract law. However, it will make it possible to appreciate the theoretical assumptions that make contracts so essential to a wider interpretation of legal systems, generally, and the contribution that the notion of a contract has made to modern public legal development, particularly.

Classifications of Contracts

Most legal systems classify contracts according to the form they assume, the relationships they infer, and the number and scope of parties included. The classifications that will be offered within this brief introduction correspond especially to the principles of contract law within the United States. However, these principles are readily transferable to other legal systems (especially, but not exclusively, among common law systems), and they provide a good basis for a comparative analysis, even in cases where the terms or principles are not precisely comparable to other systems.

Contacts often are characterized as being either "express" or "implied." Contracts that are explicitly presented and understood are called express. The most obvious example of an express contract is a detailed written document that specifies the contractual agreement. However, express contracts also can be oral, or they can be based upon the procedures of a typical sales transaction, as in the purchase of an item in a store, which is an explicit contractual arrangement (the interest in purchasing an item that has a clearly listed value, the presentation of the item to be purchased, the calculation of the sum of its worth, the payment of that sum), despite the lack of the usual formalities associated with a contractual transaction.

An implied contract occurs when the actions of one, or both, parties appear to suggest the willingness to engage in a particular contractual arrangement. A person declares, in the presence of many people, a willingness to pay a certain sum of money for someone to dig a ditch on that person's property. One of the people who witnessed that declaration proceeds to get a shovel and, with the awareness of the person who made the original declaration, begins to dig the ditch according to specifications that the first person previously had indicated. Upon completion of this task, the second person asks the first person for the previously declared sum of money—an exchange of property, in the form of labor, for property, in the form of cash. The first person has a contractual obligation, in this instance, to pay the second person, for the actions of all parties suggest both a contractual offer and a *tacit* willingness to enter into that contractual arrangement (the first person, for example, did nothing to indicate that the second person should stop the digging) upon the part of both parties. Implied contacts involve such unarticulated circumstances of actions that infer, in the absence of more formal communication, the willingness to exchange property in some manner.

An additional category, called a "quasi-contract," occurs under conditions in which a reasonable demand for compensation can be made, despite a lack of even a tacit agreement of one or the other party. A veterinarian comes to the aid of a suddenly injured animal that is held by its owner at the road side. This veterinarian may, later, demand that the second person pay a fee, in exchange for the property of professional service and expertise expended in treating the animal. Although neither party provided express or implied indication of negotiating a contractual arrangement, the circumstances present a situation where the fulfillment of such an exchange is based, instead, upon a reasonable expectation of compensation.

Contracts also can be characterized by the number of parties who engage in them. The most conventional form is termed "bilateral." As the name implies, it includes two people exchanging property. The involvement of a third person does not expand this contract to a trilateral one; instead, the third party must engage in separate bilateral contracts with the other two parties, even though the overall expectations of these transactions are, somehow, linked. Unilateral contracts involve, despite the inference of their name, more than a single person. They are based upon an offer from a single source, but directed toward anyone or, at least, anyone complying with certain conditions. The most common example of a unilateral contract is the advertising of a sales offer. A company offers to sell a certain product at a certain price to anyone who is willing to purchase it, provided they are among the first one hundred people to respond to the offer. Unilateral contracts can be even more open-ended—the social contract is conceived in such a way. They are, crudely stated, general offers made by one to all.

These characteristics provide a frame for facilitating a complete transaction. However, the modern legal concept of a contract differs from other, similar agreements or arrangements. This distinction can be made through the identification of four key elements that modern legal authorities generally insist must be present for a genuine contract to exist. Again, the American version of this legal idea will be emphasized, but its general principles correspond broadly to the image of a contract found within most other societies and their respective legal systems.

Elements of a Contract

A contract normally must include certain components, in order to be considered valid. Four elements are especially prominent. First, a contract must be based upon an "agreement." This element generally consists of two components: an "offer" and an "acceptance." The offer is an initiation of a contractual relationship, which can occur when, for example, one party declares to another party that they have an item to sell. The acceptance is a reciprocation of that offer, which can occur when the party indicates a willingness to accept the offer. This element merely is the initiation of a contract; its completion requires additional parts.

The next conventional element of a contract generally is identified as "consideration." It also consists of two components. Consideration must be premised by a "promise," which articulates the conditions that must be present for a particular contract to be fulfilled, such as an indication that a certain product, meeting certain criteria of quality, will be made available by a specified time. Likewise, the other party, for example, promises to pay a certain amount of money, by a certain time, for this product. The fulfillment of a promise occurs through "performance." Both parties actual accomplish their promises or, if unable to achieve this result, concur in an alternative to, or modification of, that result which constitutes an adjusted promise. The completion of the conditions of consideration allow a contractual arrangement to continue.

The next customary element of a contract commonly is called "capacity." This element is important, because it determines the propriety of the contractual relationship and its parties. One aspect of capacity is "standing," which is a way of expressing legal personality. A party has standing when it enjoys the legal status necessary to engage in legal relationships, including a contract. Many legal systems typically indicate standing by identifying a party as a legal "person." Standing can include individual people, organizations, companies, corporations, or associations of people. The legal system can exclude certain people, in this respect; children often are placed within this category. The property that is being exchanged through a contractual arrangement can be possessed by these "non-persons," but they are not necessarily allowed to dispose of it by themselves, although other people may engage in a contractual arrangement on their behalf.

Capacity generally also includes a component called "competence," which refers to the actual ability of the parties engaged within a contractual relationship to understand and competently make decisions related to it. People who suffer from a diminished mental state typically are deemed to lack competence, including people who may be temporarily affected by debilitating circumstances, such as having drunk too much alcohol. That person may have standing, but the judgment deemed necessary to exchange property in a fair and meaningful way is not present. Therefore, this prohibition not only protects the potential parties to a contract, but the integrity of this legal institution and the economic system that is tied to these relationships of exchange.

Capacity also can include a matter of "relevance." The parties engaged within a contractual arrangement must actually control the property that is being exchanged. One party normally cannot sell an item that belongs to someone else. An exception to that restriction can occur when a third person is designated as an "agent" of one of the parties. These agents are necessary for engaging in contracts that include a party that lacks legal standing, such as parents who negotiate a labor contract (to perform, for example, as an actor) on behalf of their child. Agents also can be authorized by persons enjoying all the elements of capacity but who prefer to have someone else engage in the contractual process for them, especially when the agent has an expertise in this sort of negotiation and legal arrangement, like professional sports and entertainment agents.

The fourth conventional element of a contract is "legality." The proposed contractual arrangement must not violate the law, in order to be regarded as legitimate. A person who sells illegal drugs and does not receive the money promised by another party for those drugs cannot expect legal relief for this problem; indeed, this contract, itself, is invalid and not only will not be enforced, but its results can be actively negated by the state. But this element also is applicable to contractual arrangements that do not violate the law but which the state determines to be contrary to the policy interests of the sovereign. Certain contracts concerning the selling of housing developments, the trading of corporate shares that affect overall economic conditions, or the proposed purchase of locations that are deemed to have historical significance for the community can be prevented through an invocation of this element. Zoning laws that affect real estate contracts are designed to provide contractual guidance according to the standards of this element. Legality provides a way for the larger society to become involved in the contractual process, by invoking the overriding sovereign claim of a "community interest," in addition to the government creation and enforcement of the rules that publicly regulate these, otherwise, "private," or civil, activities.

Contracts and Their Status

Some contractual arrangements can be ended through the mutual agreement of the parties. The basis for this termination often is arranged in advance, as part of the process of "consideration." The inability to meet certain standards of "performance" may be part of the "promise" that is resolved, in advance, by this breaking of the contract, rather than trying to enforce its consummation, or seeking alternative compensation, through a recourse to the regulatory authority of the state. These contracts conventionally are termed "voidable." This designation differs, technically, from a "void" contract, which never met the standard of legality and, so, never even qualified as a contract. Therefore, reference to a "void contract" is, actually, an oxymoron.

Typically, though, a contract that conforms to the standards indicated through these basic elements is regarded as "valid." The importance of maintaining a system for ensuring valid contracts facilitates the general success of the legal system, especially, but not exclusively, within liberal societies. But even within non-liberal systems, the concept of the contract remains the most fundamental expression of the legal relationship. Therefore, students of comparative law need to appreciate its most basic principles, even in a simplistic, introductory way.

References

Robert A. Hillman, *The Richness of Contract Law: An Analysis and Critique of Contemporary Theories of Contract Law*. Dordrecht, The Netherlands, Kluwer Academic, 1998.
Henry Mather, *Contract Law and Morality*. Westport, CT, Greenwood, 1999.
Stephen R. Munzer, *A Theory of Property*. New York, Cambridge University Press, 1990.
J. E. Penner, *The Idea of Property in Law*. Oxford, Oxford University Press, 2000.
Carol M. Rose, *Property and Persuasion: Essays in the History, Theory, and Rhetoric of Ownership*. Boulder, CO, Westview, 1994.
G. H. Treitel, *An Outline of the Law of Contract*. London, Butterworths, 1995.

CHAPTER 12

Rights and Liberties

The most dynamic legal concept of the twentieth and twenty-first centuries has been the idea of rights. This term has become part of both the legal lexicon and normal social conversation. It is a politically dynamic word, and its meaning has evolved considerably, throughout human history. It also is an extremely emotionally charged word, subject to grave misunderstanding and potential misuse. It has become, in fact, one of the most prominent considerations of contemporary global politics and an indispensable feature of all modern constitutional traditions, especially in the aftermath of the Second World War. A truly complete comparative assessment of modern law would be practically impossible without including a critical understanding and evaluation of this idea that has come to occupy the apex of twenty-first century political, social, and legal discourse.

Defining and Distinguishing Rights from Liberties

The terms "rights" and "liberties" typically are invoked interchangeably. However, they refer to two different approaches to a similar lineage. The best way to represent this distinction is through the use of the prepositions that most frequently attend one term, in contrast to the other one. People have a right *to* something, while they have a liberty *from* something. This difference is significant in terms of the necessary responses to the rights and liberties claimants regarding externally related parties. A liberty, or (using its most appropriate synonym) "freedom," from something demands a constraint. Government, other people, or other forces observe a claim to a liberty by refraining from interference. Therefore, a *freedom* of speech entails the absence of any force that prevents the claimant from exercising this sort of expression.

A *right* to speech, though, is a different proposition. A right, properly interpreted and applied, demands a positive response from external parties (usually the government) toward the party seeking to exercise the right. Therefore, a *right* of speech does not involve simply forsaking any actions that would interfere with someone's form of expression; it requires assistance in the process, such as occurs when a government makes public airwaves extensively available to political commentators, or imposes "equal time" requirements upon media sources that offer partisan editorial commentary, so persons and groups with opposing perspectives may have access to an equally effective medium of expression.

Generally, though, the guarantee of rights require an institutional response. Most assurances of due process, for example, require the establishment of a legal system that can meet that criteria. The same conditions are necessary for responding to a claim for voting rights. Therefore, this definition of rights occasionally is labeled as a "positive right," in contrast to liberties, which are occasionally called "negative rights," because they require the *absence* of response from external forces—most notably in the form of government.

The word "right" has been subject to different meanings, throughout history. It has referred to privileges that a person receives as a result of rank or office. It has referred to obligations imposed by a broader social, legal, and political order. The French word *droit* traditionally refers to law, in general, and only its more modern usage has included the contemporary translation of "right" as an alternative meaning. Modern English-speaking people often have used it in support of a sense of personal interest, expressed by such assertions as "I have a right to that job"; "I have a right to that piece of pie"; "I have a right to drive on a two-way street in either direction." In many instances, this sort of language represents not only an inaccurate use of this term, but it reflects an "inflationary" trend in the use of a language of rights. A general right to work may be argued as a human right, but the claim to a right to a particular job actually may reflect, more accurately, a belief that a person is so well qualified for that position that the normal workings of the marketplace *ought* to result, rationally, in this person being selected. The claim made upon the piece of pie may reflect a more accurate belief that the person has more merit for claiming it, rather than a true sense of absolute entitlement. The so-called "right" to drive in either direction on a two-way street really is a mere reflection of the fact that a particular statute designates a particular street for this sort of vehicular movement—a new statute could, easily, convert it into a one-way street, or designate it as a place restricted to pedestrian traffic.

The language of rights have become popular, but it also has tended to distort the meaning of this emotionally charged word. Furthermore, the terms rights and liberties have been attached to the qualifying categories of "civil" and "human" that also are frequently misunderstood and misapplied. Therefore, an accurate explanation of the conditions that constitute true rights and liberties, within the context of these two categories, is an indispensable requirement for gaining a meaningful understanding of this essential component of contemporary law and constitutionalism.

Civil Rights and Liberties

The true identification of any right or liberty depends upon its association with a condition or feature that is essential for achieving and identifying it. Another way to signify this idea is to assert that rights and liberties are grounded upon an *ontological* distinction, as explained within the chapter devoted to Western natural law. The very "being" of a party is predicated upon the principle or feature that is associated with this right or liberty. Rights and liberties, properly understood, are based upon a claim to something that, in its absence, would diminish the very identity of the party making this claim. This definition can be clarified by placing rights and liberties into two distinct categories, each grounded in distinct *ontological* identities that must be distinguished, prior to defining each category.

Civil rights and liberties constitute the more parochial of these two categories. The key for understanding this category of rights is found within the word "civil," which is derived from the Latin word *civitas*, referring to the concept of a city or, more accurately, the ancient concept of a city-state. The full member of the *civitas* is a resident of the city, from which word is derived the term "citizen." Civil rights and liberties belong, specifically and exclusively, to citizens, so that identification becomes the *ontological* source for the precise definition of this specific category.

Civil rights and liberties are grounded upon fundamental qualities that a citizen needs to function, truly, *as* a citizen. They are not simply the rights of citizens, but rights *for* citizens; without them, persons could not live and participate *as* citizens within their polity. Since citizenship is a qualification for achieving recognized standing within a polity's legal system (though standing can be achieved by certain classes of non-citizens, such as registered corporations and other organizations), civil rights also can be described as the rights that denote legal "personhood."

The ancient concept of a civil "right," though, referred to the privileges associated with the status of citizenship. The modern concept is much more intrinsically linked to the rise of the liberal state. The premier liberal value, for this purpose, has been identified as the abstract conceptualization of "property." Persons actually become designated in terms of their property—indeed, a full member of a liberal society, technically, *is* property, as explained within the chapter on Western ideology and law. A citizen, or legal "person," is distinguished particularly by the role of a property *bearer*, rather than merely a passive *possessor* of property. A frequently repeated aphorism concerning civil rights and liberties is that *all* rights are "property rights," even when they appear to be directed toward some other purpose. This axiom is based upon the theoretical ability to link every activity, within a liberal society, to some sort of "proprietary" purpose.

An example of this contention is speech. Citizens must be able to engage in speech to protect their interests, persuade other members of society, influence the political process, and participate in the marketplace, both literally, in terms of the economy, and figuratively, especially in terms of engaging in a "marketplace of ideas." But speech is the expression of an idea that constitutes, theoretically, an abstract form of "property." Furthermore, speech is employed, typically, to advance or protect a wide range of individual or shared interests, which also can be characterized, in the broad, theoretical sense, as property interests.

Thus civil rights and liberties are more specifically tied to this *ontological* premise of the liberal emphasis upon "property." They are invoked either *as* some form of property (like speech, which can be characterized as intellectual property) or in defense and advancement *of* property interests. The status and protections associated with liberal democratic citizenship can be conceived in that way. Due process rights require the ensuring of institutions and processes that allow citizens to defend themselves against the coercive power of the state. Due process also tends to include features that treat accused citizens as proprietary interests, themselves, by denying the state access to their own thoughts, information, or any personal possession, regardless of whether or not it might prove to be "incriminating." Voting rights advance the cause of limited government and the general protection of proprietary interests, especially through the influencing of public policy. Indeed, defense of one's own person *is* a defense of "property," particularly in terms of civil liberties, which seek to free citizens from the power and potential constraints of government and other forces. Privacy becomes the supreme expression of this concept of civil liberties, especially when it is described (as it was, famously, in the seminal essay on the subject by Samuel Warren and Louis Brandeis) as "the right to be let alone."[1]

Inalienable Civil Rights and Liberties

But, even in the presence of a general theoretical recognition of the premise that civil rights and liberties are the exclusive domain of property-bearing citizens, agreement on the ultimate origin, scope, and interpretive perspective of civil rights and liberties is subject to considerable variation and disagreement. Contrasts are based upon different interpretations of liberal democracy, as described within the

---

1   Samuel D. Warren and Louis D. Brandeis, "The Right to Privacy," 4 *Harvard Law Review*, no. 5 (1890), p. 19.

chapter on Western ideology and law, and the institutional expression of the state that results from the approaches to these principles and values. The earliest method for articulating civil rights and liberties originated under the influence of a "classic" liberal, or libertarian, tradition of liberal democracy.

A libertarian conception tends to emphasize civil liberties, since they are most consistent with the desire to ensure a limited government and promote individual freedom. An even more significant consequence of this approach is the way that the actual origins of civil rights and liberties are conceived and explained. John Locke described the liberal state as a creation of free, property-bearing persons who enter into a "social contract." They surrender some of their absolute personal power (specifically, the so-called "right of self-defense") and delegate it to a government which they create and legitimize. All other powers they retain, and it is these *retained* qualities that are designated as "rights." Since these civil rights (which include, semantically, liberties) originate with the persons who engage in the social contract, and since they are not derived from any external source (except, arguably, God), then they cannot be attributed to government or any other force. They are not, therefore, derived from "outside" the persons who possess them. Another way of expressing that ideal is to declare that these civil rights and liberties are "inalienable."

This distinction may seem parochial and, even, trivial, but it has a very powerful effect upon the way that people who ascribe to libertarian interpretations of liberal democracy think about their rights and liberties, and the demands they accordingly place upon their governments, in this respect. Inalienable rights and liberties are *never* given to persons by governments, the rest of society, or any other political source of authority. This sort of legal environment is shaped by this political expectation. The language of rights can be particularly inflated, and the judicial, rather than the legislative, system tends to receive a disproportionate use and attention, as political controversies often are framed in terms of a clash between policy (as shaped and enforced by government) and rights or, even, among conflicting rights claims. A libertarian approach to civil rights and liberties often envisions them as legal absolutes, especially when constitutionally expressed.

Consensual Civil Rights and Liberties

An alternative approach to the libertarian interpretation of liberal democracy is one that has been traced to the ideas of continental European political theorists, including Jean-Jacques Rousseau, in addition to utilitarian thought. This approach stresses the "democratic" features of liberal democracy, treating a concept of rights and liberties from a more collective perspective. A concept of civil rights and liberties as inalienable is expressive of a highly individualistic society; in contrast, this approach reflects a stronger sense of the cumulative identity of a self-aware political community. The philosophical movement known as "communitarianism" is derived from this perspective, and it tends to result in an interpretation of civil rights and liberties as being derived from a general consensus among the community, rather than an inalienable mandate available to, and often determined by, each separate member of that community.

This concept of rights as the product of consensual agreement has a profound affect upon the modern understanding of civil rights and liberties, especially regarding constitutional expressions of these principles. A concept of inalienable rights can be derided, within this communitarian tradition, as being offensive to the democratic sovereign and destructive of the legitimate pursuit of its goals. These civil rights and liberties impose a restriction upon the power of the sovereign which, since it is not a self-imposed limit, undermines democracy in a couple of ways. First, it encourages members of the polity to withdraw their "property" and political participation by invoking their rights and liberties and insulating themselves behind this legal shield. Furthermore, claims of inalienable rights could represent an obstructionist assertion by powerful members of society who simply use these claims as a way of protecting their vast power and preventing the community from drawing from these resources that could advance the common good.

This approach relies upon some means of being able to link specific civil rights and liberties with a demonstration of widespread recognition of this elevated status. Constitutional institutions often provide a good source for achieving this legitimacy. However, another distinction of this communitarian perspective mandates a less rigorous judicial role in the process of interpretive rights and liberties. The legislature, as the supreme expression of the sovereign will, often employs wide discretion in these matters. The definition and scope of certain civil rights often can be modified by legislative institutions as a means of reconciling them with legitimate and, often, laudable policy desires. Furthermore, some communitarian critics reject the very presence of civil rights and liberties that can be invoked in a way that would invalidate sovereign legislation. Civil rights and liberties, from this perspective, can exist only as a higher expression of sovereign will and not as a form of individual opposition to that collective will.

Modern republican interpretations of civil rights and liberties can be ambiguous, and variations of explication are possible in this respect. Neither a claim to inalienable, consensual, or, even, a rejection of a special role for civil rights and liberties are necessarily inconsistent with certain ways of conceiving and expression modern republican political and legal norms. However, that modern ideological approach, especially when absorbed within a broadly malleable liberal democratic tradition, often reserves a special role for civil rights and liberties as an essential institution of the polity. The republican emphasis upon conceiving a political community in terms of uniting distinct, component sectors and interests offers a potentially important role for rights and liberties, especially for key segments of the population who have a coherent identity but who constitute a minority of the overall community. Rights and liberties offer them (especially elite members of society) an institutional device for protecting their interests and including them in the wider scheme of republican government.

Civil rights and liberties provided the earliest opportunity for articulating this modern development. Therefore, the rise of the liberal state and the evolution of liberal democratic thought has influenced, most profoundly, the emergence of a powerful heritage of rights and liberties, generally. However, this notion of property based individual protections (developed with particular zeal during the seventeenth, eighteenth, and nineteenth centuries) is not, by far, the only option for conceiving and applying this crucial legal ideal. The atrocities of the Second World War and the challenges of a diverse, dynamic, and volatile post-modern world spurred a widespread desire to expand the reach and scope of this forceful political, legal, and constitutional legacy.

Human Rights and Liberties

The difference between civil and human rights and liberties is *ontologically* enormous. It also is subject to equally enormous misunderstanding, misuse, and vagueness. Its popularity has grown tremendously during the twentieth and twenty-first centuries, but its roots are tied to a long-established tradition of natural law, and the breadth of its appeal is not merely confined to modern Western expressions of law. Arguably, it has become the single most influential (if not, morally and politically, the most important) legal development in the world, perhaps even more than democracy. Therefore, a brief introduction to human rights and liberties as a distinct concept is undeniably crucial to a meaningful comparison of law and legal systems.

Civil rights and liberties are grounded upon an *ontological* definition of citizenship and the liberal principle of "property." In contrast, human rights and liberties, as the term implies, are grounded upon an *ontological* analysis of the human condition. Therefore, before a definition of human rights and liberties can be reached, a more fundamental definition of the essential feature that distinguished humans from non-humans is needed.

That definition can prove difficult, especially in terms of reaching consensus. Certain other animals, for example, can exhibit signs of intelligence, emotion, and interaction that are not, necessarily, distinct from the human condition. However, one quality that can be cited with a certain degree of confidence relates to human intellectual self-awareness and a capacity (indeed, arguably, an unavoidable necessity) for making choices, being decisive, and a desire to exert a certain conscious control over one's own destiny. That same principle has been described as being essential to a liberal democratic society, also, and it is called "autonomy." But it is a principle that transcends any particular philosophical tradition or culture.

This autonomous capacity confers not only a special sense of self-identity but, also, tremendous dignity upon human beings. The more persons can impose control over their own destinies, then the more options they have regarding the choices in their lives, the greater scope of decisions they are able to make, the more autonomous they become and, thus, the more "human" they feel. Those conditions and tools that advance this human autonomy become integral to the very essence of humanity, so they also become the basis for a conception of human rights and liberties.

Human rights and liberties also encompass, in an overarching manner, the realm of civil rights and liberties, since humans are, as Aristotle asserts, "political animals" who find true human expression by exercising meaningful control over their respective political environments, including in defense of their "property." But they also encompass all other things that promote human autonomy. A right to education is a good example of a human right. It is a right, because it demands a positive response from other sources (particularly government) to provide that educational infrastructure. It is, more specifically, a *human* right, because, although it does not necessarily defend or promote a "property" interest, it does provide humans with the intellectual tools they need to think critically, make decisions, and shape their future.

Human rights and liberties are dependent upon a particular philosophical tradition. Marxists, for example, might advance the concept of a "right to work" by arguing that labor is a source of fundamental human expression and identity, in addition to providing a means for expanding the options of human life and potential, so work is neither a physical necessity or economic imperative but, in fact, a source of human dignity. Other philosophical traditions identify additional and, sometimes, contrasting definitions of human autonomy, so a human rights tradition faces the supplemental burden of being widely inclusive. Additionally, human rights cannot be confined to the Western legal tradition, since it aspires to apply to *all* human beings.

An Eastern cultural concept of human rights can be discerned. Some critics have argued that the promotion of human rights and liberties constitutes a form of Western cultural "imperialism," especially since it is predicated upon an individualism that is most consistent with the domineering principles of Western liberal democracy. However, human rights can be reconciled readily with Eastern philosophical norms. A Confucian interpretation, for example, might express human rights in terms of *giri*; a ruler has a duty to respect the autonomy of subjects, especially within that sphere that falls outside their duty toward the sovereign. The ruler is expected to respect the privacy of subjects in all areas in which an intrusion upon that privacy is not mandated by the responsibilities of governance. Furthermore, one of the reciprocal duties of a ruler might be, indeed, a mandate to uphold and promote the privacy of all subjects, especially in the interest of the harmony of all.

This brief introduction can do no more than offer a suggestive and, necessarily, cursory proposition concerning the most fundamental legal, political, and philosophical definition. But the important point is that an ideal of human rights and liberties has emerged. It finds a good deal of inspiration from aspects of the natural law tradition, but it also can be tied to the fundamental assumptions and orientations of all philosophical traditions, both Eastern and Western. It also has been prompted by the practical desire to accommodate a global political community that has become increasingly interactive and that also seeks to overcome the terrible legacy of human degradation of the Second World War and the Cold War period. Indeed, this still emerging human rights heritage has been instrumental in fostering constitutional development throughout the late twentieth and early twenty-first centuries. It merits much more attention than this sort of introductory text can offer, and it has become the richest source for comparative analysis, especially among scholars and practitioners who want to appreciate, fully, the modern and post-modern evolution of law.

The Scope of Rights and Liberties

One of the most effective ways to evaluate rights and liberties is through contrasting them with their legal "opposites." Civil rights and liberties can be most effectively contrasted with the power of government, which, according to liberal democratic theory, can be ascribed to the "harm principle" of John Stuart Mill. Even from a libertarian perspective of inalienable rights, it is possible to argue that the legitimate scope of rights extends only as far as the equally legitimate borders of the governmental responsibility for protecting society from harm.

This rights/harm dichotomy finds a human rights parallel in terms of those conditions that can extend the scope of human potentiality through "power." The expression of a people in terms of their sovereignty is a particularly important aspect of that power, and it is possible to argue that human rights and liberties can be bound, legitimately, by that consideration. The most critical concept, in this respect, is the assertion that rights and liberties are overwhelmingly crucial, but never absolute. Determining the legitimate borders of this authority is one of the most important tasks of modern law, and it is a theoretical conundrum with enormously significant practical implications for all people existing under legal regimes, throughout the world.

Collective Rights and Liberties

Both the civil and human variations of rights and liberties are expressed, conventionally, in individual terms. This expression has been especially, but not exclusively, true regarding the liberal democratic origins of proprietary civil rights and liberties. An alternative expression, in collective terms, has become increasingly popular. This concept of "collective rights" should be assessed as part of the larger legal heritage of rights and liberties, especially since it poses potential implications for contemporary constitutional traditions.

Collective rights and liberties assume, by definition, the subsuming of separate, individual needs and interests. They are the rights and liberties of a group, as a consolidated entity, so all members of the group benefit from them, uniformly. But this advantage must override any individual goals, desires, or, even, rights, that individual members of the group might, otherwise, claim and enjoy. A collective right to strike for better working conditions provides an excellent example of this phenomenon. Members of a labor union decide, collectively, to exercise this right. Some members of the union vote against this action, but they find themselves in the minority. Nonetheless, the commitment they have made to this group means that this collective right prevails over an individual right or liberty regarding a desire to continue to work or to express satisfaction with current labor conditions. *All* members of the union will exercise this right to strike, including those members of the union who do not support this collective decision; otherwise, the strike and, consequently, this collective right would be ineffective, since individual workers who continue to exercise an individual right to work would nullify its effectiveness.

Collective rights also are expressed in terms of cultural and political identity. Language rights are included within its parameters, for example. The most dynamic collective rights claim involves the desire of a group to seek some form of sovereign authority over itself. This "right of self-determination" has been a dramatic modern development that was articulated and applied with particular force, following the First World War, and reinforced, following the end of the Cold War period and the collapse of the Soviet Union and its hegemony over Eastern Europe. Again, this collective right, when claimed by the group, can override an individual proclivity; members of the group who oppose this sovereign status may find themselves, nonetheless, forced to accept this political identity, once the group has achieved this collective right.

Collective rights and liberties can be a difficult concept. They are easily misidentified, for many claims regarding a collective right often constitute, actually, claims to other, legitimate political prerogatives. A claim, for example, to a "collective right to security" that overrides individual liberties of political activity really are mere expressions of the sovereign authority of the state to exercise the "harm principle." Furthermore, many so-called "group rights" to cultural identity, such as the right to use a particular language in social and political discourse, actually constitute an individual right to this benefit that is expressed, simply, in collective terms. Even the "freedom of association," as conventionally experienced, can be more accurately described as an individual liberty, since a person retains the *individual* option of joining, or not joining, an association, and the mere fact that persons have a guarantee that they may form this association does not, itself, confer any collective rights *of* this group entity, nor does it, by itself, override the individual rights and liberties of the separate members.

However, this concept has become increasingly popular. It has been embraced, particularly, by critics of the more libertarian articulations and practices of individual rights and liberties, especially in response to the effect they allegedly have in undermining collective political activity, including the individual use of judicial authority to nullify legislative policies intended to benefit society. Yet it should be emphasized that the heritage of rights and liberties originated with, and remains, overwhelmingly, an individual phenomenon. Furthermore, references to "collective" rights often are misidentifications of individual rights and liberties (a language right, for example, may actually be nothing more than an individual right to choose the use of one, or another, language for purposes of social and political discourse) or references to the sovereign powers of the state that may be imposed upon the entire polity.

Political Determination of Rights and Liberties

Anyone can make an assertion that anything constitutes a right or liberty, including the example, used previously within this chapter, of a so-called "right to drive on a two-way street in either direction." But the establishment of a genuine right or liberty requires a certain political process in response to theoretical criteria. The institutional expression of that process may differ widely among political and legal systems, but the pattern remains relatively consistent.

First, a right or liberty must be based upon a genuine "entitlement." It can be derived from a liberal principle of the necessary proprietary interests of citizens, or a more universal reference to features of human autonomy, but it must be linked to this sort of essential foundation. Second, this entitlement needs to be promoted in terms of a specific "claim" to a right or liberty that will advance the achievement of this entitlement. Finally, this claim must be recognized and affected by sovereign authority.

An example of this process is the achievement of women's political rights. This entitlement can be found within liberal appeals that women, in addition to men, are full members of society who need to protect their property interests through this political activity. It also can be found within broader appeals to the autonomous expression that women, as humans, cannot achieve without equal political participation. Subsequently, women claim a right to vote. However, this claim has no practical effect until political sovereigns acknowledge the justice of this desire and enact the appropriate political action to make it happen. The example of the United States is instructive. Women were not treated as full citizens within American society. During the nineteenth and early twentieth centuries, many activists argued that women qualify, as much as men, as property *bearers*, rather than simple property *possessors*. They used that argument as a basis for making a claim to a right to vote. But only when the legitimacy of this entitlement was accepted by the political establishment, representing the sovereign will, did this claim achieve recognition in the form of a constitutional amendment, finally enacted in 1920, that guaranteed a woman's right to vote in American elections.

This process can reflect the perspective of inalienable rights through the device of asserting that women always had a right to vote, but the American sovereign refused to acknowledge the fact until 1920. It also could reflect a consensual perspective through the device of asserting that American society needed to reach a condition of widespread acceptance of this belief in the full civil status of women as a necessary prelude to achieving this consensus of belief, culminating not just in a law but in an actual changing of the overarching constitutional order. However, the ultimate point is that just because a "right" is claimed does not mean that the claimant is, necessarily, correct. It must meet certain theoretical criteria, or the process needed to convert the "claim" into that "right" ultimately will not succeed.

Legal and Constitutional Consequences of Rights and Liberties

It is a tribute to the power of this legacy of rights and liberties that it is so vulnerable to an inflation of both language and expectations. The adoption, within international law, of covenants designed to protect and promote human rights and liberties (most notably including the United Nations Declaration of Human Rights) have been particularly impressive, even when they fail to achieve their goal. It has become practically inconceivable for contemporary states to create a constitutional order that does not include some official reference to rights and liberties, even among non-liberal and authoritarian political systems. The paramount importance of this legal ideal clearly has become firmly established.

Yet the specific understanding and application of rights and liberties can vary, widely. Traditional liberal interpretations of civil rights and liberties do not always translate readily to non-Western cultures. Even certain conventional approaches to human rights and liberties may contravene the legitimate values and beliefs of certain societies. But that fact does not nullify the significance of this legacy. Human rights and liberties have become, indeed, a universal phenomenon, although their expression often needs to be modified to accommodate alternative philosophical expressions of this ideal, such as articulating a human right, from a Confucian perspective, in terms of *giri*.

Nonetheless, rights and liberties have become an indispensable feature of the twenty-first century. Constitutions provide the source for identifying the entitlements that are the basis for their claiming and recognition and, consequently, imposing that standard upon the remainder of a political system's legal order. Comparative constitutional analysis requires an appreciation of this legacy and its true significance, especially for the purpose of gaining critical insights into the diverse examples of the world's constitutional traditions.

References

Randy E. Barnett, ed., *The Rights Retained by the People*. Fairfax, VA, George Mason University Press, 1989.
Sir Isaiah Berlin, *Four Essays on Liberty*. Oxford, Oxford University Press, 1986.
John C. Domino, *Civil Rights and Liberties: Toward the Twenty-First Century*. New York, HarperCollins, 1994.
Jack Donnelly, *The Concept of Human Rights*. London, Routledge, 1989.
Ronald Dworkin, *Taking Rights Seriously*. Cambridge, MA, Harvard University Press, 1978.
John Finnis, *Natural Law and Natural Rights*. Oxford, Clarendon, 1980.
Harold S. Lewis, Jr. and Elizabeth J. Norman, *Civil Rights Law and Practice*. St. Paul, West, 2001.
John Rawls, *A Theory of Justice*. Cambridge, MA, Belknap, 1971.
Ian Shapiro, *The Evolution of Rights in Liberal Theory*. Cambridge, Cambridge University Press, 1988.
Steven S. Stephens, *The Uncertainty of Legal Rights*. New York, Routledge, 2001.
Judith J. Thompson, *The Realm of Rights*. Cambridge, MA, Harvard University Press, 1990.
Alan R. White, *Rights*. Oxford, Clarendon, 1985.

CHAPTER 13

The Moral Idea of Law

Law is one of the most basic of all human expressions. It often attempts to encapsulate the profound images associated with the very meaning of existence, even when it represents (as most people tend to experience and regard it) the mundane features of life. That quality of law was expressed by Hillel, one of the most famous authorities of Jewish law, the Talmudic scholar and teacher of the early first century CE and a man who could well have instructed the young Jesus.

One often-related story that has been told about Hillel concerns a rabbinical student who was goaded into asking him a question. The student approached the great Jewish scholar, who was reclining beneath a tree, and asked, "Rabbi, I am told that you are capable of reciting the whole of the law while standing upon one foot—is it true?" Hillel contemplated the query for a moment and, then, replied "I believe I can." He rose from the ground, balanced himself upon one foot, and, then, said "you will love God as much as you possibly can, and you will earnestly try to love other people as much as you love yourself." Then, Hillel put down his other foot and resumed reclining beneath the tree. The student was perplexed, so he finally asked "is that all?" Hillel responded, "what do you mean?" The student persisted, "what about the books of the Torah; what about the voluminous writings of the Talmud; what about the copious writings of rabbinical commentaries; what about all the rest of it?" Hillel responded, "oh, the rest? It's just a footnote."

Law belongs to humanity; it is not merely the domain of legal professionals. Ordinances, decrees, statutes, regulations, and constitutions are enacted, after all, not by law clerks, working in professional isolation, but by politicians who live in a real, competitive, and value-laden world. Their behavior is a response to the culture, people, and political institutions surrounding them, and these features are, in turn, reflections of fundamental beliefs and values. Law should not be relayed to people exclusively through law schools or apprenticeship programs, nor should it be confined to the halls of academia. It should be part of the common body of knowledge that all members of society ought to receive, especially when they constitute, collectively, the final source of sovereign authority for a democratic polity.

Ideally, one of the most potent purposes of public education within many democratic societies is the performance of a civic duty, especially to prepare students to assume their role as citizens and sovereigns. Unfortunately, too many people often regard their education merely as a means to prepare them to acquire practical skills and enter the work force. The notion that education is a means of acquiring the power necessary to exercise their sovereign authority, together with other citizens, over the political system often seems absurdly abstract. That larger purpose of developing the capacity for critical thinking and expression as an end, in itself, often is difficult to convey to many members of society.

The additional contention that law is a vital part of that body of knowledge for people other than aspiring lawyers is an even more daunting effort, especially in terms of convincing them that this knowledge offers an effective response to the challenges of their personal, social, economic, and political lives. This book challenges the conventional assumptions about both the nature of law as a technocratic field and its relevance to the typical member of society, especially while engaged in the conventional process of education. It seeks to advance that ambitious purpose and assist people, especially (but not exclusively) higher education students, in understanding the law as an overarching public (especially political) concept that belongs to them and their world, as much, or more, than it belongs to the legal profession.

Law is more than the sum of its rules. It is the ultimate expression of politics. Indeed, it can be used to define the very polity. Public law is the realm that is most pertinent to this process. The broad legal mandate establishes the guiding principles that the political system will express and enforce, while also providing limits and constraints upon that system. Therefore, law can liberate people while, simultaneously, inhibiting them. That contradiction works particularly well within a democratic society. The ultimate role of public law (particularly in the guise of a constitutional tradition) is, in fact, the expression of a sovereign ideal. Subsequently, the nature and purpose of that law depends upon the sovereign source of its fundamental values that serve as its, and the polity's, foundation. Indeed, the self-conscious identity of sovereign authority cannot be maintained without the law. Likewise, law cannot exist without a sovereign to inspire it and define it.

Laws of human communities that do not conform to its moral precepts are regarded as lacking a substantive quality of law. However, the legitimacy of law is determined by the ability to articulate and enforce it, rather than upon its moral authority. These divergent expectations are not as contradictory as they might seem, and a critical theoretical understanding of the idea of law would allow an observer to make and, even, explain that distinction. Likewise, the criteria and workings of any emanation of law, from constitutional articles to contractual clauses, are not random acts of power but rational expressions, grounded upon these same, broadly theoretical considerations. It is that quality that makes public law particularly representative of all aspects of a legal system. Therefore, in order to determine the inner reasoning that makes the components of a legal system consistent with each other, it is necessary to determine those foundational criteria that make a political system's public law truly "public."

All legal institutions are part of a broad tradition of law. These essential concepts of law that are found within constitutions may not be apparent, for example, but that presence remains, nonetheless, real. Therefore, emphasis needs to be placed upon the underlying cultural and ideological values that define, and direct the development of, a body of law, prior to evaluating any single specific legal clause. The occasional disdain of some legal practitioners who regard law as an exclusive process and treat social science and humanist critiques as "soft" and lacking in intellectual rigor may be correct to the extent that their ability to work within their respective professions is not dependent upon that body of knowledge. Nonetheless, the legal documents they process are, in fact, political instruments that provide the foundational expression of the political ideals and values of a society that are derived, in turn, from philosophical experience and discourse. Ultimately, that knowledge is needed, even for professional purposes, since, without it, law can degenerate into an arbitrary exercise in random force that lacks consistency, predictability, and relevance to the polity that it is suppose to serve.

Constitutions are supreme declarations of the political culture of any society, so they can provide the best venue for attaining this level of understanding. Furthermore, constitutional law frames the political society in which all of its members exist, so a failure to understand law at that level can result in a failure to appreciate and, thus, control one's own political destiny. That lack of autonomy can be the most dehumanizing consequence of a parochial approach to law that abdicates responsibility for interpreting and shaping it to a limited number of juridical elites.

Laws are not simply technical instruments of bureaucratic means, nor are they mere tools of enforcing raw political power. Laws derive their meaning from constitutions, which are, in turn, philosophical declarations of the will and fundamental values of the sovereign. Professional jurists inevitably draw upon broad theoretical beliefs in the interpretation of public law, even when claiming a fierce attachment to a so-called legal "objectivity." But a pivotal difference exists between a jurist applying her or his personal values to a legal analysis and making a distinct connection between those invoked principles and the particular history, culture, and developing beliefs of a politically defined community.

The relationship between law and politics has not been overlooked by legal practitioners. In fact, it is the average citizen who is much more guilty of that oversight and who should be particularly jealous of that prerogative. Still, complacency at all levels appears to be the norm, especially when it is sanctioned by an even more pervasive belief in the irrelevance of a widespread appreciation of law by all members of society. That attitude further supports the stereotype of a law that is "merely process" and subject to complicated rules that exist within a world of their own, rather than the world around each person who experiences it.

That "objective" and "morally neutral" approach to legal interpretation is, ultimately, untenable. It is practically impossible to divorce the influence of political, economic, social, and moral influences (including ones derived from philosophical beliefs and values of the political community) from the law. Nonetheless, law often appears to be treated in exactly that way. This book has attempted, therefore, to illuminate the essential concept of law as a means of stripping it of superfluous obscurity, confusing technicalities, and moral ambiguity. It has reduced it to its components, so it can be rebuilt within the minds of everyone affected by it, giving them the tools to control it, their society, and their lives. If this book has advanced that purpose in even the slightest way, it has achieved a measure of success.

References

Aristotle, *Basic Works*, Richard McKeon, ed. New York, Modern Library, 2001.
Gabriel A. Almond and Sydney Verba, *The Civic Culture Revisited*. Newbury Park, CA, Sage, 1989.
Kirstin Hastrup, ed., *Legal Cultures and Human Rights: The Challenge of Diversity*. Boston, Kluwer, 2001.
Antero Jyränki, *National Constitutions in the Era of Integration*. The Hague, Kluwer, 1999.
Giovanni Sartori, *The Theory of Democracy Revisited*. Chatham, NJ, Chatham House, 1987.
Mortimer Sellers, ed., *The New World Order: Sovereignty, Human Rights, and the Self-Determination of Peoples*. Oxford, Berg, 1996.

Bibliography

John A. Abbo and Jerome D. Hannan, *The Sacred Canons: A Concise Presentation of the Current Disciplinary Norms of the Church*. St. Louis, Herder, 1957.
Nicholas Abercrombie, Stephen Hill, and Brian S. Turner, *The Dominant Ideology Thesis*. London, George Allen and Unwin, 1985.
Gabriel A. Almond and Sydney Verba, *The Civic Culture Revisited*. Newbury Park, CA, Sage, 1989.
Andrew Altman, *Critical Legal Studies: A Liberal Critique*. Princeton, NJ, Princeton University Press, 1990.
James G. Apple and Robert P. Deyling, *A Primer on the Civil-Law System*. Washington, Federal Judicial Center, 1995.
St. Thomas Aquinas, *Summa Theologiæ*, Thomas Gilby and T. C. O'Brien, trans. and eds. Cambridge, Blackfriars, 1966.
Aristotle, *Basic Works*, Richard McKeon, ed. New York, Modern Library, 2001.
Aristotle, *The Politics*, Ernest Barker, trans. and ed. Oxford, Clarendon, 1952.
Charles Auerbach, *The Talmud: A Gateway to the Common Law*. Cleveland, Western Reserve University Press, 1952.
John Austin, *Lectures on Jurisprudence*, Robert Campbell, ed. London, John Murray, 1885.
John Hamilton Baker, *The Common Law Tradition: Lawyers, Books, and the Law*. London, Hambledon, 2000.
Randy E. Barnett, ed., *The Rights Retained by the People*. Fairfax, VA, George Mason University Press, 1989.
Jeremy Bentham, *The Works of Jeremy Bentham*, John Bowring, ed. Edinburgh, William Tait, 1843.
Sir Isaiah Berlin, *Four Essays on Liberty*. Oxford, Oxford University Press, 1986.
John H. Berthrong and Evelyn Berthrong, *Confucianism: A Short Introduction*. Oxford, Oneworld, 2000.
Thomas J. Biersteker and Cynthia Weber, eds., *State Sovereignty as Social Construct*. Cambridge, Cambridge University Press, 1996.
John Eaton Calthorpe Blofeld, *Taoism: The Road to Immortality*. Boston, Shambhala, 2000.
Daniel J. Boorstin, *The Mysterious Science of the Law: An Essay on Blackstone's Commentaries*. Chicago, University of Chicago Press, 1996.
Sir George Bowyer, *Introduction to the Study and Use of the Civil Law*. London, Stevens, 1874.
J. L. Brockington, *The Sacred Thread: Hinduism in Its Continuity and Diversity*. Edinburgh, University of Edinburgh Press, 1996.
Masaji Chiba, ed., *Asian Indigenous Law: Its Interaction with Received Law*. London, KPI, 1986.
Chin Kim, *Selected Writings on Asian Law*, Littleton, CO, Rothman, 1982.
Hugh Collins, *Marxism and Law*. Oxford, Oxford University Press, 1984.
James A. Coriden, *An Introduction to Canon Law*. New York, Paulist, 2000.

René David and John E. C. Brierley, *Major Legal Systems in the World Today*. New York, The Free Press, 1978.
Rodolphe A. J. De Seife, *The Shari'a: An Introduction to the Law of Islam*. San Francisco, Austin and Winfield, 1994.
John C. Domino, *Civil Rights and Liberties: Toward the Twenty-First Century*. New York, HarperCollins, 1994.
Jack Donnelly, *The Concept of Human Rights*. London, Routledge, 1989.
Jerry Dupont, *The Common Law Abroad: Constitutional and Legal Legacy of the British Empire*. Littleton, CO, Rothman, 2001.
Ronald Dworkin, *Law's Empire*. Cambridge, MA, Harvard University Press, 1986.
Ronald Dworkin, *Taking Rights Seriously*. Cambridge, MA, Harvard University Press, 1978.
Daniel J. Elazar, *Constitutionalizing Globalization: The Postmodern Revival of Confederal Arrangements*. Lanham, MA, Rowman and Littlefield, 1998.
Daniel J. Elazar, *Exploring Federalism*. London, University of Alabama Press, 1987.
Thomas Peter Ellis, *Welsh Tribal Law and Custom in the Middle Ages*. Aalen, Scientia Verlag, 1982.
Daniel Engster, *Divine Sovereignty: The Origins of Modern State Power*. DeKalb, IL, Northern Illinois University Press, 2001.
Palmer D. Evans, *Common Law Forms of Pleading and Practice*. Chicago, Callaghan, 1931.
John Finnis, *Natural Law and Natural Rights*. Oxford, Clarendon, 1980.
George P. Fletcher, *Rethinking Criminal Law*. Oxford, Oxford University Press, 2000.
Lon Fuller, *The Morality of Law*. New Haven, CT, Yale University Press, 1964.
Murray Forsythe, ed., *Federalism and Nationalism*. Leicester, University of Leicester Press, 1989.
Carl J. Friedrich, *Trends of Federalism in Theory and Practice*. London, Pall Mall, 1968.
Gaius, *The Institutes of Gaius*, William M. Gordon and O. F. Robinson, trans. and ed. Ithaca, NY, Cornell University Press, 1988.
James K. Gaynor, *Lawyers in Heaven*. Philadelphia, Dorrance, 1979.
Edward L. Glaeser, *Legal Origins*. Cambridge, MA, National Bureau of Economic Research, 2001.
Max Gluckman, *Politics, Law, and Ritual in Tribal Society*. Oxford, Blackwell, 1965.
Wael B. Hallaq, *Authority, Continuity, and Change in Islamic Law*. Cambridge, Cambridge University Press, 2001.
H. L. A. Hart, *Punishment and Responsibility: Essays in the Philosophy of Law*. Oxford, Clarendon, 1995.
Kirstin Hastrup, ed., *Legal Cultures and Human Rights: The Challenge of Diversity*. Boston, Kluwer, 2001.
Martin van Hees, *Rights and Decisions: Formal Models of Law and Liberalism*. Dordrecht, The Netherlands, Kluwer Academic, 1995.
Robert A. Hillman, *The Richness of Contract Law: An Analysis and Critique of Contemporary Theories of Contract Law*. Dordrecht, The Netherlands, Kluwer Academic, 1998.
Paul Q. Hirst, *On Law and Ideology*. Atlantic Highlands, NJ, Humanities, 1979.
Wesley Newcombe Hohfeld, *Fundamental Legal Conceptions*, Walter Wheeler Cook, ed. New Haven, CT, Yale University Press, 1964.

Honghe Liu, *Confucianism in the Eyes of a Confucian Liberal: Hsu Fu-kuan's Critical Examination of the Confucian Legal Tradition*. New York, Peter Lang, 2001.
Hsin-chung Yao, *An Introduction to Confucianism*. Cambridge, Cambridge University Press, 2000.
Margaret C. Jasper, *The Law of Personal Injury*. Dobbs Ferry, NY, Oceana, 2000.
Antero Jyränki, *National Constitutions in the Era of Integration*. The Hague, Kluwer, 1999.
Leo Katz, Michael S. Moore, Stephen J. Morse, eds., *Foundations of Criminal Law*. New York, Foundation, 1999.
Preston T. King, *Federalism and Federation*. Baltimore, Johns Hopkins University Press, 1982.
Harold J. Laski, *Authority in the Modern State*. Hamden, CT, Archon, 1968.
Harold S. Lewis, Jr. and Elizabeth J. Norman, *Civil Rights Law and Practice*. St. Paul, West, 2001.
Peter Lewisch, *Punishment, Public Law Enforcement, and the Protective State*. Vienna, Springer-Verlag, 1995.
Frederick K. Lister, *The European Union, the United Nations, and the Revival of Confederal Governance*. Westport, CT, Greenwood, 1996.
Denis Lloyd [Lord Lloyd of Hampstead], *The Idea of Law*. London, Penguin, 1987.
Martin Loughlin, *Public Law and Political Theory*. Oxford, Clarendon Press, 1992.
Catharine A. MacKinnon, *Toward a Feminist Theory of the State*. Cambridge, MA, Harvard University Press, 1989.
C. B. Macpherson, *The Life and Times of Liberal Democracy*. Oxford, Oxford University Press, 1989.
Frederic William Maitland, *The Forms of Action at Common Law: A Course of Lectures*, A. H. Chaytor and W. J. Whittaker, eds. Cambridge, Cambridge University Press, 1971.
Susan Marks, *The Riddle of All Constitutions: International Law, Democracy, and the Critique of Ideology*. Oxford, Oxford University Press, 2000.
Henry Mather, *Contract Law and Morality*. Westport, CT, Greenwood, 1999.
Brian E. McKnight, ed., *Law and the State in Traditional East Asian Law*. Honolulu, University of Hawaii Press, 1987.
Arthur Taylor Von Mehren, *The Civil Law System: Cases and Materials for the Comparative Study of Law*. Boston, Little, Brown, 1977.
John Henry Merryman, David S. Clark, and John O. Haley, *The Civil Law Tradition: Europe, Latin America, and East Asia*. Charlottesville, VA, Michie, 1994.
Susan Millns and Noel Whitty, eds., *Feminist Perspectives on Public Law*. London, Cavendish, 1999.
Charles de Secondat, Baron de Montesquieu, *L'esprit des lois*. Paris, Librarie Médici,1948.
Bradford W. Morse, ed., *Aboriginal Peoples and the Law*. Ottawa, Carleton University Press, 1989.
Stephen R. Munzer, *A Theory of Property*. New York, Cambridge University Press, 1990.
Alexander Nékám, *Experiences in African Customary Law*. Edinburgh, University of Edinburgh Centre of African Studies, 1966.
John K. Nelson, *Enduring Identities: The Guise of Shinto in Contemporary Japan*. Honolulu, University of Hawaii Press, 2000.
Edward C. Page and Michael J. Goldsmith, eds., *Central and Local Government Relations: A Comparative Analysis of West European Unitary States*. London, Sage, 1987.

Leslie Palmier, ed., *State and Law in Eastern Asia*. Brookfield, VT, Dartmouth Publishing, 1996.
Evgenii Bronislavovich Pashukanis, *Law and Marxism: A General Theory*, Barbara Einhorn, trans., Chris Arthur, ed. London, Pluto, 1989.
A. K. Pavithran, *Substance of Public International Law*. Madras, Rajendran, 1965.
J. E. Penner, *The Idea of Property in Law*. Oxford, Oxford University Press, 2000.
Poh-Ling Tang, ed., *Asian Legal Systems: Society and Pluralism in East Asia*. Sydney, Butterworths, 1997.
Sir Frederick Pollock, *The Law of Torts*. London, Stevens and Sons, 1916.
Frank Pommersheim, *Braid of Feathers: American Indian Law and Contemporary Tribal Life*. Berkeley, University of California Press, 1995.
James Provost and Knut Walf, and Marcus Lefébure, eds. *Canon Law—Church Reality*. Edinburgh, T. and T. Clark, 1986.
John Rawls, *A Theory of Justice*. Cambridge, MA, Belknap, 1971.
John D. Rayner, *Jewish Religious Law: A Progressive Perspective*. New York, Berghahn, 1998.
Isabelle Robinet, *Taoism: Growth of a Religion*, Phyllis Brooks, trans. Stanford, CA, Stanford University Press, 1997.
Heinrich Rommen, *The Natural Law: A Study in Legal and Social History and Philosophy*, Thomas R. Hanley, trans. St. Louis, Herder, 1959.
Carol M. Rose, *Property and Persuasion: Essays in the History, Theory, and Rhetoric of Ownership*. Boulder, CO, Westview, 1994.
Lawrence Rosen, *The Justice of Islam: Comparative Perspectives on Islamic Law and Society*. Oxford, Oxford University Press, 2000.
Giovanni Sartori, *The Theory of Democracy Revisited*. Chatham, NJ, Chatham House, 1987.
Mortimer Sellers, ed., *The New World Order: Sovereignty, Human Rights, and the Self-Determination of Peoples*. Oxford, Berg, 1996.
Ian Shapiro, *The Evolution of Rights in Liberal Theory*. Cambridge, Cambridge University Press, 1988.
Marshall S. Shapo, *Basic Principles of Tort Law*. St. Paul, West, 1999.
Moshe Silberg, *Talmudic Law and the Modern State*, Ben Zion Bokser, trans, Martin S. Wiener, ed. New York, Burning Book, 1973.
Thomas W. Simon, *Law and Philosophy: An Introduction with Readings*. New York, McGraw-Hill, 2001.
K. S. Singh, ed., *Tribal Ethnography, Customary Law, and Change*. New Delhi, Concept, 1993.
Peter Stein, *Roman Law in European History*. Cambridge, Cambridge University Press, 1999.
Steven S. Stephens, *The Uncertainty of Legal Rights*. New York, Routledge, 2001.
Mark Tebbit, *Philosophy of Law: An Introduction*. New York, Routledge, 2000.
Judith J. Thompson, *The Realm of Rights*. Cambridge, MA, Harvard University Press, 1990.
G. H. Treitel, *An Outline of the Law of Contract*. London, Butterworths, 1995.
James W. Tubbs, *The Common Law Mind: Medieval and Early Modern Conceptions*. Baltimore, Johns Hopkins University Press, 2000.
Bertus de Villiers, ed., *Evaluating Federal Systems*. Cape Town, Juta, 1994.
Max Weber, *The Religion of India: The Sociology of Hinduism and Buddhism*, Hans H. Gerth and Don Martindale, trans. and ed. New Delhi, Munshiram Manoharlal, 1992.
Lloyd L. Weinreb, *Natural Law and Justice*. Cambridge, MA, Harvard University Press, 1987.

Alan R. White, *Rights*. Oxford, Clarendon, 1985.
Konrad Zweigert and Hein Kötz, *An Introduction to Comparative Law*, Toney Weir, trans. Amsterdam, North Holland, 1977.

Index

A

administrative law, 117
Aquinas, Saint Thomas, 15-16, 86, 87, 88
Aristotle, 14, 40, 86
Auden, W. H., 2-3
Austin, John, 17, 19, 116

B

Bentham, Jeremy, 19
Blackstone, Sir William, 65
Buddhism, 30
Burke, Edmund, 47-48
Byzantine Empire, 70, 71-72

C

canon law, 71, 85-88
China, 24-27
Christianity, 36, 85-86
    Anglican, 85, 88
    Orthodox, 85, 88
    Roman Catholic, 15, 48, 71-75, 85-88
civil law systems, 69-82
    historical development, 69-75
    judicial systems, 75-77
    legal education, 77-78
    legal procedures, 90-93
    sources of law, 79-81
citizenship, 135-136, 139
commercial law, 117-118
common law systems, 53-66
    historical development, 54-57
    judicial systems, 57-58
    legal education, 58-60
    legal procedures, 60-63
    sources of law, 63-65

confederal systems, 109-110
Confederate States of America, 109-110
Confucianism, 24-27, 29, 141, 145
Confucius, 24-27, 26-27, 28
conservatism, 46-49, 114
constitutional law, 5-6, 113, 117-118, 122, 123, 138, 141, 142, 145, 149
contract law, 127-131
contracts, 127-131
    bilateral, 128
    elements, 128-129
    express, 127
    implied, 127
    quasi, 127
    unilateral, 128
criminal law, 115, 118-119

D

Dworkin, Ronald, 65

E

Eastern law, 9-11, 23-33, 141, 143
    comparative perspective, 9-11, 23-33, 44-45
    Confucian approach, 24-27, 29, 141, 145
    Hindu approach, 31-33
    Legalist approach, 27-29
    Taoist approach, 29-30
Engels, Frederick, 44
England, 54-56, 60, 66, 72, 106
European Union, 110

F

family law, 119
federal systems, 107-108

feminism, 49-51
feudalism, 36-38, 39, 125
Finnis, John, 65
France, 73-74, 78

G

Gaius, 14, 70
Germany, 71-72, 75
Great Britain, 41, 43, 57, 106
Greece, ancient, 10-11, 13
Grotius, Hugo, 16

H

Han Fei-tzû, 27-28
Hart, H. L. A., 65
Hegel, Georg Wilhelm Friedrich, 43
Henry II, king of England, 54
Hillel, 90, 147
Hinduism, 31-33
Hobbes, Thomas, 47

I

ideology, 35-51, 137, 149
    conservatism, 46-49
    feminism, 49-51
    liberal democracy, 41-42, 113, 114-116, 121, 122, 136-138, 139, 140, 141-142, 144
    liberalism, 39-42, 49, 50, 116, 118, 119, 122, 135-137, 139
    Marxism, 42-46
    medieval antecedents, 36-38, 39, 48, 125
India, 24, 31
Islam, 91-93

J

Japan, 24, 29-30
Jesus, 14, 85
Judaism, 88-91, 147

Justinian the Great, Byzantine emperor, 15, 70-71

L

Lao Tzu, 29-30
law, 1-7, 147-150
    general theory, 1-3
    moral purposes, 4-5, 147-150
    objectivity and neutrality, 3-4
Legalism, 27-29
liberal democracy, 41-42, 113, 114-116, 121, 122, 136-138, 139, 140, 140, 141-142, 144
liberalism, 39-42, 49, 50, 116, 118, 119, 122, 135-137, 139
Locke, John, 40, 116, 137

M

MacKinnon, Catharine, 65
Marx, Karl, 42, 43-44
Marxism, 42-45
Mencius, 27, 28
Mill, James, 19
Mill, John Stuart, 142
Mohammed, 91-92, 93

N

Napoléon I, emperor of France, 73
natural law, 10-17, 135
    historical development, 14-17
    origins, 10-13
Nuremburg Tribunal, 16

P

Paul of Tarsus, Saint, 85
penal law, 120-122
Phillips, Owen Hood, 65
Plato, 14
positive law, 17-20
    historical development, 18-20

origins, 17-18
Posner, Richard, 65
private law, 119-120, 129
property law, 116-117, 121, 125-128, 135-136, 139, 144
    personal property, 126
    real property, 125-126
Prussia, 74
public law, 116-119, 148-149

R

Rawls, John, 65
religion and law, 85-94
    canon law, 71, 85-88
    Talmud, 88-91
    Shari'a, 91-93
rights and liberties, 133-145
    civil, 135-139
    collective, 142-144
    consensual, 137-139
    distinction, 133-134
    human, 139-141
    inalienable, 136-137
    political determination, 144-145
Rome, ancient, 14-15, 36, 69-71
Rousseau, Jean-Jacques, 40, 137-138
rule of law, 113-114

S

Savigny, Friedrich Carl von, 74
Scotland, 74, 106
Shammai, 90
Shari'a, 91-93
Shintoism, 30
Sophists, 14
sovereign arrangements, 17-18, 19, 105-110, 149
Soviet Union, 42, 46
state, 114-116, 133
Stoics, 14
Switzerland, 109, 110

T

Talmud, 88-91
Taoism, 29-30
tort law, 122-123
tribal law, 36, 97-103
    decision making, 101-103
    leadership, 99
    patterns, 98-99
    property, 100-101

U

Ulpian, 14, 70
unitary systems, 106-107
United States, 57, 66, 107, 109, 110, 127
University of Bologna, 71-72, 73
utilitarianism, 19-20, 137-138

W

Wales, 106
Western law, 9-20, 23-24, 32-33, 94, 135, 137
    comparative perspective, 9-10, 32-33
    natural law, 12-17
    origins, 10-11
    positive law, 17-20

TEACHING TEXTS IN LAW AND POLITICS

David Schultz, *General Editor*

The new series Teaching Texts in Law and Politics is devoted to textbooks that explore the multidimensional and multidisciplinary areas of law and politics. Special emphasis will be given to textbooks written for the undergraduate classroom. Subject matters to be addressed in this series include, but will not be limited to: constitutional law; civil rights and liberties issues; law, race, gender, and gender orientation studies; law and ethics; women and the law; judicial behavior and decision-making; legal theory; comparative legal systems; criminal justice; courts and the political process; and other topics on the law and the political process that would be of interest to undergraduate curriculum and education. Submission of single-author and collaborative studies, as well as collections of essays are invited.

Authors wishing to have works considered for this series should contact:
>Peter Lang Publishing
>Acquisitions Department
>275 Seventh Avenue, 28th floor
>New York, New York 10001

To order other books in this series, please contact our Customer Service Department at:
>800-770-LANG (within the U.S.)
>(212) 647-7706 (outside the U.S.)
>(212) 647-7707 FAX

or browse online by series at:
>WWW.PETERLANGUSA.COM